# Praise for *Connecting with*

*'Flavia has a natural and intuitive connection to the faery realms. She speaks in a way that is easy for all to understand, and gives a very real insight into the magical faery world, where communication with the fae is effortless.'*

KAREN KAY, EDITOR IN CHIEF, *FAE* MAGAZINE

*'The world of the fae needs you, it needs me and it needs its guardians. Flavia is one of those defenders; a guide to the world of faerie magic who is as magical as the beings she champions. This book brings knowledge, it brings wisdom, it brings connection and it brings heart and soul as it brings the world of the fae into your life. I loved spending time, through the pages, with Flavia and the faerie folk!'*

DAVID WELLS, AUTHOR OF *YOUR ASTROLOGICAL MOON SIGN* AND *QABALAH*

*'Reading this book is like stepping into a beautiful dream: but one from which you awaken to the endless possibilities that harness the true essence and magic of faery folklore.'*

PROFESSOR RONALD HUTTON, PROFESSOR OF HISTORY, ENGLISH FOLKLORE, BRISTOL UNIVERSITY

*'Flavia is a true visionary and advocate of the old ways. Her in-depth knowledge of the fae is timeless and thought provoking as she weaves her magic throughout this book.'*

BARBARA MEIKLEJOHN-FREE, THE HIGHLAND SEER AND AUTHOR

*'Fairy enthusiasts will love this practical guide which helps you connect to the magic of the 'little people' to transform your life. Flavia's tone is warm, wise and informative. A must-have for your spiritual book collection.'*

KATY MOON, COMMISSIONING EDITOR, *SPIRIT & DESTINY* MAGAZINE

# CONNECTING WITH THE

# Fairies

## Made Easy

# CONNECTING
## WITH THE

Fairies

Made Easy

## DISCOVER THE MAGICAL WORLD
## OF THE NATURE SPIRITS

## FLAVIA KATE PETERS

**HAY HOUSE**

Carlsbad, California • New York City
London • Sydney • New Delhi

**Published in the United Kingdom by:**
Hay House UK Ltd, The Sixth Floor, Watson House,
54 Baker Street, London W1U 7BU
Phone: +44 (0)20 3927 7290 • Fax: +44 (0)20 3927 7291
www.hayhouse.co.uk

**Published in the United States of America by:**
Hay House Inc., PO Box 5100, Carlsbad, CA 92018-5100
Tel: (1) 760 431 7695 or (800) 654 5126
Fax: (1) 760 431 6948 or (800) 650 5115
www.hayhouse.com

**Published in Australia by:**
Hay House Australia Ltd, 18/36 Ralph St, Alexandria NSW 2015
Tel: (61) 2 9669 4299; Fax: (61) 2 9669 4144
www.hayhouse.com.au

**Published in India by:**
Hay House Publishers India, Muskaan Complex, Plot No.3, B-2,
Vasant Kunj, New Delhi 110 070
Tel: (91) 11 4176 1620; Fax: (91) 11 4176 1630
www.hayhouse.co.in

This book was previously published as *Fairies* (*Hay
House Basics* series); ISBN: 978-1-78817-020-8

A catalogue record for this book is available from the British Library.

ISBN: 978-1-78817-262-2
E-book ISBN: 978-1-78817-278-3

13 12 11 10 9 8 7 6 5

Interior illustrations: 9, 10, 33, 34 Flavia Kate Peters; all other illustrations:
Montage by Celine Boivin (Image Evgeniia Litovchenko/shutterstock).

Printed in the United States of America

*Time to dance with nature*
*and keep the magic alive!*

# Contents

# List of Exercises

# Foreword

From a young age, I always sensed that there was life in the very air around me. I spent so many of my childhood days in nature and learning about the wildlife of the Scottish countryside, but I always had a strong feeling that, for all I could see, there was something else beyond my human senses.

In this book, Flavia brings the magic of my childhood wonders to life and makes me believe that, for all the heaviness of this human world in our current times, there is still a magic that exists. This is the magic of the light world, which coexists with ours. A world that has always been there and shall awaken when we need it most. That time is now.

*Fairies* is a book that allows the mind to journey between two worlds and remember that there is much more to life than we first perceive, and Flavia – or 'Flavalicious' as I call her – has truly captured this in her enchanting work. I urge all who read this book to search their psyche to reawaken their magical self and allow it to come out and play. When we release our tight grasp on logic and serious thinking, the child within us can be free.

**Gordon Smith**
**Medium and author of** *The Unbelievable Truth*
**and** *Intuitive Studies*

# Introduction

*As I enter within this magical ring,*
*my heart is open and ready to sing*
*songs of the wood, words of the fae,*
*who guide me in and show me the way.*
*I call on them this very eve,*
*whose mystique and mystery together doth weave.*
*May power be granted this very night,*
*as I share my new gifts, for 'tis only right.*
*With arms outstretched to the magical ones,*
*I give honour and thanks, and now it is done.*

Many of you reading this may feel an affinity with fairies. You may have felt the call of their magic since childhood. Deep within, you may feel drawn to return to the old ways, the old days when magic abounded and the human and fairy worlds respected each other and worked in harmony to ensure the natural balance of all things.

It is time to heed the call. For the world of the fae has sounded a great alarm. It is time to wake up and acknowledge that this is a world that is falling out of balance. And we share it with another realm.

So you may now be feeling your mystic self stirring. Glimmers of ancient memories may be surfacing – of moonlight bathing in deep blue pools, of weaving through forests, feeling the warmth of sunbeams falling through lush green leaves, and of dancing through golden cornfields to celebrate the harvest. To the fairies, it was only yesterday when they played with you, my friend. They miss you and the magic that you exude when you allow yourself be the free spirit you naturally are.

It is time to take on the sacred role of fairy pathwalker and redress the balance. A fairy pathwalker is someone who hears the whispers of spirit on the breeze, who welcomes the rains, glorifies in the heat of the sun and connects with the nourishment of the earth beneath their feet. They embrace each season, rejoicing at every new bud during the first stirrings of spring, the harvest abundance that summer supplies, the falling leaves of autumn and deep dark mystery that accompanies the winter months.

A fairy pathwalker's heart sings at the mere notion of magic. They have an affinity with the ways of natural healing and believe in an Otherworld of mystical beings. This is the world of fairy – a shining world within our own, a world of rock spirits, crystal spirits, guardians of lakes, streams and oceans, spirits of forests, meadows, mountains and even towns and cities, all supporting the ways of nature through the working of miracles and magic.

Many of us have been brought up on fairy tales and 'make-believe'. We are no strangers to glittery fairy dust, magic wands, toadstool fairy rings and the ever-popular tooth fairy! However, fairies are far from the sparkling characters of children's bedtime stories. These mystical creatures are neither fantasy nor fiction – they are very real beings of nature. Fairies are in waterfalls, in streams, in meadow, garden and forest. They are present in every flower, every leaf and blade of grass, every rock and stone. They are waiting for you in the caves and hills, the skies and oceans. Will you acknowledge them and take a step sideways to become a part of their magic?

But where will this journey of mystery lead, you may ask? The pathway is uncertain, and there may be pitfalls and losses along the way, but you can be assured that wherever the fairy realm takes you, it will always be for the highest good.

The Earth needs our help and the fae are calling us to revere the ways of our ancestors, who worked in union with these very real nature spirits. The world has changed and seems to spin at a much faster pace, with high-tech gadgets, transport and the like. But embracing the fairy kingdom does not mean you have to lose all that you know in this day and age. In return the fairies will offer their assistance so that you can heal, create and thrive in this very modern world.

When you recognize that fairies are the beings who work in conjunction with the elements that govern each and every one of us, that they are the magic behind all that is alive on this wondrous planet, you are brought back into alignment with the natural world. Then your own manifestation and healing abilities are ignited, and you are able to change how you experience life and embrace the magic that is all around. And that is the way to bring the world back into balance.

The true mystic keeps a foot in both worlds, for they know the reality of both. It is time to introduce the world that has been hidden for too long back to the other, which seems to have lost its way without its magical counterpart.

So rejoice, for the magic that your soul craves is about to be revealed... Delight in the wonder of who you are and step into a fairy ring, search for pixies, swim with the mer-folk and hug a tree. Magic is everywhere and in everything. Go discover it! Enjoy every precious moment. By taking steps along the fairy path and working in conjunction with the mysteries of nature, you will find the overall outcome will be more satisfactory than you could ever imagine – and you're guaranteed to experience great fun and a huge sprinkle of magic along the way!

# Chapter 1

# Awakening to Magic

*A magical kingdom exists in my mind,*
*of wonder, enchantment and all of that kind.*
*If I just close my eyes and count up to three,*
*I see fairies and pixies waiting for me.*

Do you remember when the world seemed magical? When you skipped through an enchanted forest and played dress-up and make-believe? Perhaps that wonderful feeling has waned as you have faced the responsibilities and challenges of life. Maybe the joy has dimmed and a veil of cynicism now cloaks your senses.

Fairies are calling you to reawaken and tap into the magic that is all around you. It is time to see once more through the eyes of a child, with wonder and awe. As your spiritual sight opens at the hint of a magical touch, you will discover a hidden world that you have long forgotten. Time to re-establish your connection and step into the mystery that beckons you. As a new magical energy surrounds you, go grab your dreams and reach for the stars. The world of fairy is poised to support you.

*Once upon another time,*

*entranced, you skipped and sang in rhyme.*

*Mystic sight was lost – so tragic.*

*A spell now doth restore your magic!*

## Once upon another time...

The very first time that I saw a fairy was when I was no older than two years. As I peered up through the large hollowed-out trunk of an ancient oak tree, I saw a tiny light flitting about in the dark. Though small, it was the brightest light I had ever seen. I was mesmerized and instinctively knew it was a fairy. So that was it, my mission was to search for fairies! And that is what I set about doing for my entire childhood.

I was brought up in rural Berkshire, England, and lived with my family on the edge of vast woodland. As a young child I would wake early and sneak into the woods to sit with the trees, knock on the little ready-made fairy doors that were embedded into the tree trunks and leave food offerings for the 'little people'. Idyllic days were filled with dreaming, meditating and sometimes actually seeing the 'fair folk'. As the years went by, I built up an amazing relationship with these magical beings, having spent hours in the woods communing and connecting with them, learning from the natural world that surrounded me.

## 'Fairy' or 'faery'?

So what are they and what should they be called?

Fairies are beings made up of high-vibrating energy of light. They resonate at a higher frequency than we do, which is why it is difficult for us to see them. However, they can appear to us by slowing down their vibrations, and at certain times of the day, such as the magical hours of sunrise, dusk, noon and midnight, we are more likely to connect with them and see them. They reside on the astral plane, which is an energetic frequency we can connect with through imagination, wishes, invocation and spells, and portals from this world to theirs exist through pools of water, at the crossings of ancient paths and in circles of mushrooms or flowers. It is at these places that we may see them in our physical world – if we are lucky! (*Check out Chapter 7.*)

The word 'fairy' derives from Middle English *faierie*, which is a direct borrowing from Old French *faerie*, meaning 'the land', 'realm' or 'enchantment', which is in turn derived from the ancient word *fae*. The term refers to the ancient realm of nature spirits and the light and dark of the natural world.

There has been many a discussion of how the word should be spelled. 'Fairy' and 'faerie' are both used by historians and artists who connect deeply with all aspects of the fae. I ordinarily favour the spelling 'faery'. However, 'fairy', a spelling that was shaped in Romantic and Victorian literature, is most definitely the more modern, Disney-recognized version and is understood across the world, and so for that reason I am using that spelling throughout this book, with an occasional 'fae', or something equally appropriate, thrown in from time to time.

Other collective names for fairies are the 'shining ones', 'fair folk', 'little people', 'good people' and *Sidhe* (Shee).

## Fairy history

Fairies have been written about throughout history and are mentioned in ancient texts such as Homer's *Iliad* and *Odyssey*. In the days of ancient Greece, gods and goddesses were worshipped and the minor deities were recognized as the spirits of nature.

Stories of sprites and fairies abound across the world, and fairies have played a part in Oriental, Arabian and Asian cultures. Ancient Norse folklore includes tales of elves, Lorelei and other such beings, and in Ireland there are the *Sidhe*, who reside in mounds and barrows.

Like in many other cultures, the ancient Celts made fairies an important part of everyday life and treated them with deep reverence. It was general protocol to leave small gifts of food or milk out for them as a mark of respect and gratitude. For our ancestors knew that fairies had the power to bestow a bountiful harvest or bring destruction to the entire crop.

It was also believed that elves spread diseases, and if someone was ill they were said to be 'fairy taken'. Fairies were also accused of stealing babies and leaving fairy children in their place. These were called 'changelings' and were often spotted because they had an unusual 'fae' appearance or something different from the original child.

Horseshoes were placed over doorways to keep fairies away, for it was common knowledge that they could not tolerate iron, as it counteracted magic, and for protection purposes, never an ill word was spoken of the spirits of nature.

However, the fairies' supernatural powers were often called on for help in finding items, curing illnesses, seeing the future and bestowing blessings. People would seek out the wise woman of the community or a fairy 'doctour' who had the ability to connect with the fairy realm and heal with the assistance of these magical beings.

During the Middle Ages, the prevailing religion in the West taught that fairies were fallen angels, and the worship of nature was stamped out – or so the pagan-fearing perpetrators thought! Any connection with fairies had to be made in secret, until the Industrial

Revolution of the late eighteenth century, when the land was first destroyed in the name of 'progress' and pollution filled the air. Then the nature spirits had to step up a gear and needed humankind to hear their plight, so the fae came back into the minds and hearts of those who could sense them.

More people are accepting that fairies are real nowadays, and a new train of thought is changing the way that they are perceived. It is wonderful that those who feel a connection with the magic and mystery of the fairy realm can now stand proudly and publicly, whilst fun and laughter are enjoyed at the many fairy festivals and balls that are popping up across the UK and USA. Joy is, after all, the highest vibration and a much sought-after gift of the fae!

Even though it is fun to dress in tutus, stripy tights and fairy dust, the fairy realm is not to be disrespected or taken lightly, however. For every good fairy, there has to be a 'not so good' fairy, for nature teaches us that there is shadow and light within everything. So there are fairies who help plants to grow and fairies who assist in the decaying process. These are the fairies who are perceived by humans to be malevolent in character. But they all have their role, and there are many avenues of the fae to be explored and honoured. Seek out the magic within and the magic around you will surely show itself.

## Exercise: Opening your heart to the fae

We can connect with fairies at any time, especially when we are relaxed or out in nature. So, invite them in and allow them to help you to shine...

❖ Sit in a quiet place in nature, or next to a potted plant or crystal if you can't get outside.

❖ Now bring your focus to your heart chakra, the energy centre of your heart.

❖ Breathe deeply in and out.

❖ Now, as you inhale, breathe in *love*.

❖ And then exhale *love*.

❖ As you continue to breathe love in and out, imagine a fairy appearing before you.

❖ Take notice of what they look like, every detail.

❖ Now breathe love towards them.

❖ As you inhale, they breathe love back to you, so inhale their love.

❖ Now breathe your love back, and as they receive your love, they breathe love back to you.

❖ Continue this heart breath back and forth until you feel your heart chakra opening up to the fairy in front of you and to the fairy realm.

❖ When you have finished, thank the fairy and leave a gift, such as bread and honey, out for the fairies, in gratitude for your new relationship with them. (They like anything sweet.)

Your heartfelt presence and gift of love have been readily accepted. As have you, into the heart of Fairyland.

Your life will never quite be the same.

## Fairies and elements

Even though the fae are a different race from humankind, the Earth is still their home. Their purpose is to build all that is needed to support this world and to create it physically. Everything that we see in the natural world has been built by them. How amazing is that?! Their job is to nurture, grow and support the balance of this planet – and that includes us!

The fairy race is made up of many familiarly named beings such as gnomes, elves, dwarves, leprechauns, goblins, fauns, flower fairies, mermaids, fire spirits, pixies and many more. Countries across the world claim their own fairies and nature spirits and have names for each accordingly, such as Germany's Nix and Nixie and the Yōsei of Japan.

Each fairy type is assigned to one of the four basic elements – Earth, Air, Fire and Water. These work in harmony with one another and with the fifth element, Spirit, which runs through everything that is alive, including the other elements, to create and sustain all life on Earth.

The elements are the root of all existing matter and cannot exist without the workings of the fairy realm. They are the physical manifestations of the fairies' existence, made manifest from their realm, known as the Otherworld, or Fairyland.

Exploring the forces of nature involves reconnecting with the elements on a metaphysical and spiritual level. For each has a powerful meaning and is associated with energies that we can call upon for personal or magical assistance.

Earth maintains our logic and common sense and keeps us grounded and stable.

Earth

Fire is the motivating driving force that fuels our strength, courage and passion for life.

Fire

Air brings aspiration and inspiration and enhances creativity.

Air

Water governs our emotional wellbeing and our intuitive/psychic development.

Water

## Elementals

The powers and influences of each of the basic four elements are embodied in elementals. Elementals are specialist fairies, guardians of one of the four elements, and their task is literally to make that element work. They are the power behind it and are made of its very fabric.

It is believed that it was the Swiss alchemist Paracelsus, in the Middle Ages, who gave these spirits their names, although Empedocles, in the fifth century BCE, was the first known person to suggest that the world was created from four elements, and in the third century CE the Neoplatonists associated specific spirits with each element.

## Elemental guardians

These are the principal elemental guardians of the fairy realm:

### Gnomes

The guardians of the element of Earth are the Gnomes. These are the nature spirits who toil away at the soil, sifting through it to ensure it is nourishing, so that insect species can live in it and plants grow from it. Without the help of the Gnomes, we would have no plants or trees, no fruits, vegetables or salads to eat. The Gnomes provide us with a place to reside in, to call our home.

### Sylphs

The guardians of the element of Air are the Sylphs. These are the wispy, whispering fairies who bring messages on the winds. If you look up into the skies and readjust your eyes, you can see them as tiny pinpricks of light dancing on the breeze. Their role is to purify the air so that all loving beings who walk and grow on the Earth can breathe easily. Without these fairies of Air, we could not survive here on Earth.

## Salamanders

The guardians of the element of Fire are the Salamanders. They exist purely in the etheric world until they are summoned to this earthly existence via a matchstick, a lighter or an electrical appliance. They are lizard-like in appearance, red, orange and yellow in colour, and can be seen in the shapes of flames – no fire can exist without them!

## Undines

The guardians of the element of Water are the Undines. These are the nature spirits of wherever water exists – lakes, rivers, pools, wells, oceans and even the rain. Their role is to nurture and protect the animals and plants that reside in these bodies of water, as well as the water itself.

## Working with elementals

Fairy and magical practitioners work with elementals, inviting them into sacred space and treating them, of course, with the utmost respect. Understanding the make-up of each elemental and the properties of their element gives the basics for natural magic and alchemical workings:

- *Earth* elementals are concerned with the physical world, with growth, formation, strength and health.

- *Air* elementals are concerned with movement, communication, the psychic senses, inspiration and the powers of the intellect.

- *Fire* elementals are concerned with passion, transformation, purification and energy.

- *Water* elementals are concerned with the ebb and flow of life, tranquillity, purification, cleansing, scrying and the emotions.

Combine this with understanding the seasons and their festivals and you will find the pathworkings of the fae will open up to you in ways that you may not even deem possible!

## Fairy festivals of the year

In nature, the year is made up of four seasons. It is the sun that marks the seasonal changes and so they are honoured by celebrating four solar festivals. Cross-quarter and equinox celebrations are marked by fire festivals, and together the eight festivals of the seasons form the Wheel of the Year.

Our ancestors recognized and followed the wheel, for their very existence depended on the elements providing the right amount of rainfall, sunshine, wind and nutritious soil for a good harvest. They understood that it was the elementals who were behind the workings of the elements, and so were sure to appeal to the good side of the nature spirits and appease the rest.

Each of the festivals reflects the state of nature at the time, what is happening in the agricultural calendar, and the physical and spiritual effects the time of year has on humankind. Whatever the season, these are times for counting our blessings and for giving thanks to the nature spirits, as well as to the Goddess who continues the circle of what we call life on Earth, in her triple aspect of Maiden, Mother and Crone.

## Imbolc

**Traditional dates:** 1–2 February in the northern hemisphere; 1–2 August in the southern hemisphere

*The Maiden; innocence, purity; sowing the dream and giving birth to the inner child*

Imbolc is a time of purification in preparation for the coming year and is portrayed as the young virgin Maiden aspect of the Celtic Triple Goddess. She is the young girl awakening to womanhood just as nature begins its fertility cycle.

This is a time of emergence as new shoots appear from the ground, early flowers begin to blossom and we begin to witness the renewal of life. Daylight hours finally start to become noticeably longer at this time and we see the birth of the very first lambs as the ewes start to lactate.

This was an important time for our ancestors here in the northern hemisphere, as fresh milk once again became available, meaning the difference between life and death after the cold, harsh scarcity of winter. At Imbolc today it is still a pagan tradition to pour fresh milk on the ground to honour the Earth fairies and to ensure fertility for the coming season in the agricultural communities.

This is the time to sow new ideas, make plans and begin creative projects.

### Imbolc incantation

*'Neath a layer of soft white snow
doth a single flower grow.
The Goddess stands in Maiden form,
shining through this very dawn.
New fruits stir her virgin womb,
awakening from winter's tomb
She calls to you to now be free,
explore each possibility.
For this is when to seed your dreams,
No matter how hard and tough life seems,
they will come true – it's time to trust.
Be one with nature, don't fight or thrust.
Take the cup she offers you,
that's filled with fresh milk from a ewe.
Embrace the year with open eyes.
Magic awaits – nature tells no lies.*

## Ostara

**Traditional dates:** 21–22 March in the northern hemisphere; 21–22 September in the southern hemisphere

*The Maiden matures; from darkness to light; signs of growth and discernment*

When we are aligned with the natural world, we can embrace and honour the new creative power that is stirring throughout nature at this time. Ostara heralds the Spring Equinox – a time of balance between light and darkness, a day of equilibrium. This is a good time to look at what needs balancing in your life, what you wish to gain and what you wish to banish. It is also a time for honouring new life and is the festival that has been 'borrowed' by Christianity as Easter. So, think hatched eggs, baby chicks and all the fresh promise of spring.

The seeds planted at Imbolc need time to be nurtured deep within the Earth, and even though seedlings may now be appearing, they are not yet in full bloom. Ostara is a time of incubation, of the development of any projects, wishes, spells and dreams into which we have breathed energy. It is a time for patience. That which we cannot see needs to happen first, in the background, under the surface. So we need to wait, trust and allow the natural order of things to take place. The timing will be perfect.

### Ostara incantation

*'Tis the first stirring of spring.*
*New beginnings doth it bring.*
*Drink of what it represents –*
*new life, growth and expectance.*
*So what's the hurry and the gloom?*
*Your seed is safe within her womb.*
*The fairies work behind the scenes*
*to manifest your goals and dreams.*
*Wait and trust now are the key,*
*for life will bloom most readily.*

## Beltane

**Traditional dates:** 1–2 May in the northern hemisphere; 31 October in the southern hemisphere

*The Mother; fertile minds, bodies and souls; giving birth to our ideas and soul's knowing*

Beltane is a time of the blending of energies of the feminine and masculine to celebrate the sacredness of sexuality. The Goddess takes the God as her lover, in order to give birth to the full bloom of nature during the summer months to come. Nature is fully honoured in the fresh bright flowers, grasses and leaves that are now pushing through. It is an abundant time of year – a great celebration for the fairy realm.

This is the one age-old yearly pagan celebration that continues to this day. Villagers gather to eat together and sup ale as they are treated to traditional Morris dancing and a May Queen is chosen. Local children weave ribbons in and out as they dance around a decorated maypole. This is a phallic symbol representing the traditional rituals that were once carried out to promote fertility for livestock and people alike. Beltane is known as a fire festival, and great fires would blaze from the hilltops as a sign of protection, while others would be lit for couples to leap over hand in hand before running into the woods to consummate their union.

This is a time when the goals that were set at the beginning of the year come to fruition, when projects take off and relationships bloom. We have sown our seeds at Imbolc and now the Goddess, through her union with the God, gives birth to the idea. At Beltane it springs into reality, and continues to grow as the year progresses.

### Beltane incantation

*With fires lit across the land,*
*a couple leaps whilst hand in hand*
*to mark their union and this rite,*
*for they know tonight's the night!*
*As they run through darkened wood,*
*and find a grassy glade, they should*

*remember well who is around,*
*for bands of fairies all surround*
*the couple. As they consummate,*
*the fairies cheer and seal the fate*
*of plants and flowers, shrubs and trees,*
*whilst the God's upon his knees*
*impregnating the mother to be,*
*and sowing deep his natural seed.*
*And so, in time, the Goddess will birth*
*the magic that's nature on this Earth.*

## Litha

**Traditional dates:** 21–22 June in the northern hemisphere; 21–22 December in the southern hemisphere

*The Mother glorified; the celebration of light; being in our full glory*

This is the sun festival of Litha, or the Summer Solstice, which is when the sun is at its highest point in the sky.

This is a time of year when the veil between worlds is torn down. Fairy rings of mushrooms, toadstools and flowers can be found, and those with an open heart are invited inside them to connect with the magic of the fae.

This is a time of intensification, of focus, development and determination as we become stronger and claim the personal power we are aiming for. We may be entering unfamiliar territory, but the light of the sun will highlight the path, and we can borrow the sun's strength and warmth as we embrace the Mystery.

### Midsummer fairy ring invocation

*I call on the magic of Midsummer's Eve,*
*which mystique and mystery together doth weave.*
*May power be granted this very night*
*as I share my new gifts, for 'tis only right.*
*With arms outstretched to the magical ones,*
*I give honour and thanks, and now it is done.*

## Lammas

**Traditional dates:** 1 August in the northern hemisphere; 22 February in the southern hemisphere

*The Mother matures; gratitude for earthly, physical sustenance*

Lammas, or Lughnasadh, marks the first harvest of the year. It is the gathering in of the grains and the celebration of the sun god Lugh, aka John Barleycorn, who is cut down in his glory, only to rise again the following year. This is a time of feasting, a time of plenty and a time of acknowledging the cycle of life, death and rebirth.

By Lughnasadh, the seeds planted earlier in the year have grown into an abundant crop and the harvest has been reaped. This is looked upon as a time of opportunity and good fortune, for these are the carefree days of summer. Dreams have come to fruition and are ripe for the picking. It's time to reap the rewards and to appreciate and bless everything that comes our way.

### Lughnasadh invocation

*Today the wheel of the year doth stop*
*at Lammas – time to reap the crops*
*that were sown earlier this year.*
*Celebrate the harvest cheer*
*of wheat, of cereal, of the grain.*
*Store it safe, before the wane.*
*John Barleycorn is now cut down*
*in his prime, but look around,*
*for Lugh the sun god shines from high*
*over the fields, from the sky.*
*From Mother Earth we now are blessed,*
*toil now over, soon can rest.*
*But from the sow, what did you reap?*
*Is it good work? What have you earned?*
*Of the lesson, what is learned?*
*May the magic of this day*
*bless you now in every way.*

## Mabon

**Traditional dates:** 21–22 September in the northern hemisphere; 21–22 March in the southern hemisphere

*The Crone; the art of contemplation explored; self-sufficiency of mind, body and spirit*

Mabon celebrates the Autumn Equinox, when daylight and darkness are in balance before the darker days of winter set in. This is time of going deep within to reflect on the months beforehand, count our blessings and give thanks for the abundance that has been bestowed upon us through the year thus far.

At this time of balance and the acknowledgement of the fruit harvest, we are reminded that we too are a part of nature. Therefore it is harvest time for us, too.

### Exercise: Mabon balance

Reach into your very own storehouse to seek the balance within. If you're feeling restless, emotional or out of sorts, it's time to restore the balance in your life.

❖ What seeds did you plant in your life earlier this year?

❖ Have they come to fruition?

❖ What do you need to bring in, or release, in order to move forward?

❖ Embrace any aspects of yourself that are devoid of light and eliminate only that which does not serve you, with gratitude and lessons learned.

❖ Once balance is achieved, rest and enjoy the fruits of your personal harvest.

---

### Mabon incantation

*Autumn's upon us, here at last,*
*a time to reflect upon the past,*
*on the year that seems to have flown.*
*Dreams were planted, now they have grown.*
*Mabon gives us darkness and light,*
*the perfect balance of day and night,*
*and so we look deep down within*
*to check our equilibrium.*
*Look back on past hurts, lessons learned,*
*and use them so you won't get burned.*
*It's important to shine out far and wide*
*and to honour your shadow side,*
*for both together make you whole –*
*the two as one complete your soul.*
*Light two candles, one black, one white,*
*representing your joy and plight.*
*Eliminate all you do not need,*
*but keep what you have to succeed.*

*The harvest's in, we give great cheer
and thanks for an abundant year.*

## Samhain

**Traditional dates:** 31 October in the northern hemisphere; 30 April in the southern hemisphere

*The Crone revered; respecting our ancestors; healing our hurts*

Hallowe'en conjures up images of ghosts, pumpkin lanterns and children shouting, 'Trick or treat!' as they hungrily hold out bags for sweets. Traditionally called Samhain, this was a Celtic celebration of summer's end. Fires were lit on the night of 31 October, and villagers would burn crops and animals to share them with their gods and goddesses and to give thanks for the bounty of the harvest.

The Celts believed that the souls of the dead were set free from the Underworld for that night. Some would be welcomed and others feared, so costumes and masks were worn for protection from these spirits.

Samhain is still considered a time of reflection on and connection with those who have left this world for the other. It is also a time to look at where we ourselves have journeyed from and to during the year. The Goddess, in her triple form, has become the Crone, and we are invited to draw on her wisdom from deep within, as she cradles us during the dark months to come, enabling us to release all that no longer serves us.

As the veil between worlds is at its thinnest at Samhain, we are more able to see and connect with the world of fairy and spirit at this time.

### Samhain incantation

*Cauldrons boiling, lanterns shining,*
*ghouls and ghosts, groans and whining,*
*parties sweep across the land,*
*children, adults, hand in hand.*
*Times of fun, but must remember,*
*as fires burn bright and glow with embers,*
*our ancestors who walked before.*
*We honour thee and ask for more*
*wisdom, tools, to help us be*
*the wise amongst us. Let us see*
*through the thin veil this very night.*
*Protection in place – no need for fright –*
*so we welcome you and all you bring.*
*Go deep inside and look within*
*to shed the old, a shamanic death,*
*embraced and centred with steady breath,*
*inviting in now life anew.*
*The Goddess calls for it to be you.*
*Through the year from Maiden to Mother,*

*the end is now, to feel the other.*

*In her glory stands the Crone.*

*Don't be afraid to stand alone.*

*This sacred path leads you to be free.*

*Go forth in strength – so mote it be.*

## Yule

**Traditional dates:** 21–22 December in the northern hemisphere; 21–22 June in the southern hemisphere

*The Crone fades; the returning sun; exploring the essence of our being*

The season of winter sees the festival of Yule as a time when our ancestors and the fairies would gather to welcome the return of the sun. At the Winter Solstice the sun appears at its weakest, having waned in strength since its peak at the Summer Solstice six months earlier. But then it starts to become stronger as it heads towards the summer months once again. The birth of the sun – the light of the world! Great cheers ring out in celebration!

And the new king is heralded! Celtic tradition tells of a great battle that plays out twice a year between the mighty Holly King and the majestic Oak King. At the Summer Solstice, the Holly King wins and stands proud through to Yule, when he is cut down in his prime by the Oak King, who then presides over the months until their next battle in summer.

**Yule incantation**

*Fairy folk tiptoe soft*
*across the land of snow and frost,*
*towards a holly tree at Yule.*
*'Tis time to cut it from its rule,*
*for this battle the Oak King wins*
*and he will lord it over the months of spring*
*and in the morn turn to the sun,*
*who is born again – the light has won.*
*Each year the sacred wheel doth turn.*
*Now Yuletide's here, 'tis our concern*
*to celebrate with joy and mirth,*
*May bells ring out for 'peace on Earth'!*
*So place the logs upon the fire*
*and make wishes of your heart's desire.*
*Honour the flames that warm the cool*
*with blessings to one and all this Yule.*

## SUMMARY

- Fairies are beings who resonate at a higher frequency than we do.

- They are the builders of nature.

- It is possible to see them at times when the veil between their world and ours is thin.

- Our ancestors respected and honoured these nature spirits.

- Elementals are fairy guardians of the four basic elements of Earth, Air, Fire and Water.

- Understanding the properties of these elements is the basis of fairy magic.

- The guardians of Earth are the Gnomes.

- The guardians of Air are the Sylphs.

- The guardians of Fire are the Salamanders.

- The guardians of Water are the Undines.

- The Wheel of the Year is a calendar of festivals celebrating the change of the seasons.

## Chapter 2

# Fairy Connection

*When you wish upon a star,*
*seven points to who you are.*
*Protection placed, respect is key.*
*Honour fairy sanctity.*

Whenever we work with magic, it is vitally important that we protect ourselves. In fact, it is good practice to call in protection every day, whether we are consciously working with the fairy realm or not.

## Grounding

Before partaking in any spiritual work, be it meditation, invocation or any other form, you must 'ground' yourself. This is so that you are anchored in your body and remain connected to this Earth realm.

Going outside into nature and standing barefoot on the ground will instantly ground you and connect you to the Earth. Or, wherever you are, you can imagine strong roots growing down from the soles of your feet and burying themselves deep in the ground. Try it with the following exercise.

## Exercise: Grounding

❖ See in your mind's eye strong roots growing from the soles of your feet deep into the ground.

❖ Watch as your roots grow stronger and longer, going deeper and deeper into the ground, until they reach the centre of the Earth.

❖ Now visualize a huge crystal in the centre of the Earth. Take note of what it looks like and allow your roots to wrap themselves around it.

❖ Now breathe up the crystalline energy through your roots, breathe up the Earth magic and allow it to surge through every cell, every vessel, every part of your being.

You are now grounded and ready to connect to the fairy realm.

## Protection

In order to connect to the world of the fae, it's important to be a clear channel, which means being free of negativity and fear. You can make sure you are clear by protecting yourself against unwanted energies from other people (including psychic attacks), negative thought forms and also lower-vibrational energy that has become stuck in locations such as old buildings or places where a traumatic event has taken place.

Drawing a circle around yourself, whether physically or in your mind's eye, is a strong form of protection. Simply imagining a bubble of the brightest white light surrounding you will also immediately give you the protection that is required.

Other ways to put protection in place include visualizing a circle in front of you, or drawing one in the air with your power finger (the index finger of whichever is your dominant hand). See it growing to a little bigger than you and then step into it.

Or you may wish to use the following visualization, which will ground, centre and protect you.

## Exercise: Protection, grounding and centring ceremony

❖ Stand with your feet slightly apart and firmly on the ground. In your mind's eye, see roots growing down into the Earth below you (*as explained above*) and allow them to anchor you firmly to our dimension.

❖ Feel the strong and grounding Earth energy as you connect with the element of Earth.

❖ Now you become aware of a soft breeze caressing your body – the fairies of Air are surrounding you. Breathe in deeply. Feel and welcome the precious life-giving air entering your lungs.

❖ You become aware of a light, refreshing rain falling upon you. Embrace the fairies of Water, who have come to cleanse and purify you.

❖ A fluffy white cloud moves in the sky to reveal the sun in all its glory. The guardians of Fire are beating down their burning rays upon you. Feel the delicious warmth nurturing and healing your body.

❖ With the power of all four elements connecting with every part of you, feel yourself merging with each one of them.

❖ Draw on the strength of this energy. Feel the power surge though every part of you as you raise your arms.

❖ Stand like a star and feel your spirit soar.

❖ You are the Earth, the Air, the Fire, the Water and Spirit.

❖ Now see yourself encircled by a protective energy.

You are now grounded, centred and fully protected, and ready to take up any magical work.

## Sacred symbols

### The pentagram and pentacle

In fairy magic, all the elements – Earth, Air, Fire and Water and the etheric element of Spirit – can be called upon for specific spells. Each of these elements is represented in the ancient magical symbol of the five-pointed star, the pentagram.

Putting a circle around the star protects the five elements and the magical user, and this sacred symbol is called a pentacle. Wise ones and magical practitioners used it for protection and for casting spells (for the highest good and with harm to none) for centuries, until sadly it came to be seen as a sign of evil.

I can assure you that the pentacle is a sign of good, of connection with nature and the natural magic of which we are a part. Whenever we use it for magical purposes, or imagine being encircled by it, we have complete protection.

The pentacle

### The fairy star

The fairy star is similar to the pentacle and is used for protection and connection to the Otherworld in fairy and Celtic-based traditions. Instead of having five points, like the pentacle, it has seven, which represent:

| Point | Element | Focus | Higher Self |
|---|---|---|---|
| 1. The sun | Fire | Life, regeneration, divine spark | Power, determination |
| 2. The forest | Earth | Fertility, abundance, stability | Wisdom, growth |
| 3. The sea | Water | Womb, blood flow, emotions | Harmony, tranquillity |
| 4. Magic | | Natural and complex magic | Alchemy, glamour |
| 5. The moon | | Triplicate of the Goddess, cycles | Powers of the mind |
| 6. The wind | Air | Imagination, creativity, movement | Commitment, truth |
| 7. Connection | Spirit | Interconnection, divinity, unification | Life-force, oneness |

The fairy star

The fairy star is a gateway to the Otherworld. Each point is an entrance to the fairy realm, leading us in the right direction and giving us access to the fairy pathway.

I often wear a fairy star in the form of a necklace. It gives me daily protection as well as a natural connection to the magic that is within and all around.

## A fairy altar

When we work with fairies, it is really important to honour them, as well as the seasons and elements. This shows them our commitment to them and to our roles as fae guardians of this planet. The perfect way to do this is to create a fairy altar.

Altars have been used in temples and sacred landscapes since ancient times. When an altar is the focus for fairy ritual and sacred intent, it becomes a sacred space that holds the magical activity of the fairy pathwalker and the fairies themselves. It is also a magical focal point to have in our home – whenever we look at our altar, we immediately connect with the mystical energies it represents.

## Creating a fairy altar

An altar doesn't have to be anything grand, so don't worry if you don't have the room! It can be a table with a cloth on it in a quiet corner, a mantelpiece, a window sill or a bathroom shelf. It doesn't matter, as long as you have set the right intention.

Once you have found your perfect altar, you will need to find items to represent each element. Here are some ideas.

To represent Earth:

- a black, brown or green candle

- a bowl of soil from your homeland or a favourite sacred site

- White Californian sage – for purification and cleansing

- crystals

- stones

- a plant pot

- dried flowers

To represent Fire:

- a red candle (the lit flame)

- a picture of the sun

- an ornament of a dragon, phoenix or Salamander

To represent Air:

- a yellow candle

- a lit incense stick

- feathers (naturally fallen, found in nature)

- bells

- wind chimes

To represent Water:

- a blue candle

- water from a holy place (such as Chalice Well at Glastonbury in the UK)

- a chalice/goblet (to represent Water or to hold water itself)

- seashells

- a picture of the ocean or sea animals

Including all four elements/elementals on your altar ensures balance in all aspects of nature when honouring the natural world or fairy realm or doing all-round spell work.

It is always a good idea to keep a pentagram or fairy star on your altar too, for protection and connection. This can be in the form of a pendant or a picture, or why not make one yourself from natural materials?

I usually adorn my altar with small fairy figurines, including dragons and mermaids. You may wish to add a picture or two of an elemental being, the woods, a meadow or the ocean and/or scatter pine cones or leaves over the surface of your altar. Include whatever you feel represents the magic of nature for you.

You may also find that you wish to work with a specific element and elemental on certain issues and want to create an altar to reflect that. Each element and elemental offers its own special magic that you can harness and use effectively, as you will find in the next four chapters.

## Seeing and sensing fairies

*Seeing is believing* to the minds of humankind. But sadly we have got it all topsy-turvy. For *believing* is the key to magic. From the moment you believe, miracles happen.

Fairies may not make themselves known by appearing visually, however. They are often quite shy, or don't feel the need to slow down their vibrational frequency. But they may do so if we have done something special for them or if they particularly wish to make themselves known to us. This is usually the only way we get to see a fairy.

This happened to me whilst I was running a fairy workshop one day. The participants were sitting in a fairy ring in a beautiful courtyard setting. As I was taking them on a meditation to connect with the fae, I looked to my right and noticed two very interested fairies watching. They were both quite tall, I thought, for fairies, and one had extremely long legs, like a rag doll. Internally, I heard their sweet voices asking permission to watch, and I told them they were very welcome.

If you're of the sensitive kind – and you most likely are if you are reading this book – you may feel the presence of fairies through a change of energy, such as a feeling of bliss, a tingling down one side of your body, or even a physical push or poke! Often fairies dance on the top of people's heads. This may feel quite spidery, so be careful not to knock any fairies off if it tickles!

Often fairy lovers block their sight by trying too hard to see fairies. Stop trying to focus and you may catch sight of a fairy out of the corner of your eye, or perhaps in the form of a spark or a flash of light.

Sometimes fairies want to catch the attention of those they really want to work with. They may send butterflies, dragonflies or even frogs to them, for these creatures hold fairy energy. Other signs may include being given a stone or a crystal, having a relevant book jump out at you, receiving a fairy-related gift from a friend or finding small items going missing or something you thought was lost mysteriously reappearing.

My sweet and thoughtful friend Debbie has great compassion for the elemental realm, and we met for a cup of tea and a chat one day so that she could tell me about an environmental project she had organized. She had initially met with resistance, but was pleased to report that volunteers had now signed up, due to her perseverance.

As she reached into her shiny new handbag to show me a leaflet with the details, she looked surprised and pulled out her hand. As she opened her clenched fist, a beautiful ruby earring was revealed. She gasped, telling me that this was part of a pair she had lost years ago. She had searched high and low and had always felt they were a great loss. So how could this earring have been in a handbag that had only been bought the previous week?

Still reeling from her find, she slipped her hand back into the bag and pulled out another ruby earring, which completed the pair. We just knew that the fairies had returned her special earrings in return for what she was doing to help them and the planet.

## Imagination

If you need your finances healed, or a flow of abundance in your life, fairies are often happy to assist. They are wonderful teachers, for all they do to bring something into reality is to imagine what they want and it is created for them in an instant.

I was given this information during a Fairy Reiki healing session. As I was working with my client, a mermaid showed up in my mind's eye. Her presence told me that my client needed work on an emotional issue, as mermaids are connected to the element of Water. I then saw the mermaid visualizing plants in the ocean as already fully grown and whole, before they'd actually physically manifested. I realized that this was how the fairies lived, worked and brought about all that they desired. We can do the same, if we follow their example.

When you were younger, how often were you chastised by an elder for sharing dreams and visions from your imagination? When you were told, 'Oh, it's just in your imagination,' how did you feel? We know ourselves how real our imagination can be. It wasn't given to us by our Creator just for looking at pictures in our minds when we are bored. No! Our imagination is the portal to the Otherworld, to the fairy realm. It is through our imagination that we truly connect with fairies.

Whatever we see in our imagination can be instantly accessed by the fairies, for our thoughts are seen in the Otherworld. So, know that this form of connection can be as strong and as real as you wish. Just be mindful about what you are visualizing!

Sometimes it's fun to play with fairies in this way. For example, if you imagined yourself with gossamer wings and an acorn hat, they would see you that way instantly. They love this kind of play and would laugh!

This is a great way to build up a relationship, for fairies enjoy laughter and playing with energies. This is what magic is! It's manipulation of energy – and fairies are our best teachers!

## Exercise: Imagining

❖ Take a moment now and imagine yourself in some way or other, just for fun, and *know* that the fairies can see it.

❖ See, in your mind's eye, their reaction to whatever you've imagined and allow that to form a bond between you.

### Asking for assistance

Trusting our visualization and manifestation abilities is key to bringing about our dreams and desires. Then, through asking for assistance and taking guided action, we can bring those dreams into reality – with the fairies' help of course!

## Exercise: Asking for fairy assistance

There are several ways you can ask:

❖ Ask out loud.

❖ Ask in your mind.

❖ Write your request down and keep it on your altar, tuck it in your purse or bury it in the earth.

❖ Sing about your desires in song.

❖ Make your requests in the form of a rhyme.

However you do it, once you have asked the fairies, watch out for signs. These will often come from nature, perhaps in the form of an animal, the direction of a breeze or the shape of a cloud.

When we work with the fairy realm, our ability to notice and understand what's happening in the natural world around us, and how we are interconnected, will expand.

## Fairy offerings

As fairies have proven to me, working with and trusting in their ability to provide is a very powerful way to create what we want in our lives. In return for any assistance they have given me, I always leave a token of my appreciation out for them, such as a piece of bread and honey, a tot of mead or a piece of chocolate.

Fairies consume these gifts by breathing in their essence, rather than taking them physically. You will always know when a fairy has accepted an offering, as you will notice that the life-force of the food or beverage has completely disappeared.

## Fairy mystic awakening

Fairies are calling to us to honour the ways of our ancestors. The ancient mystics worked with the flow of the universe and recognized that when we operate in this way we re-ignite our natural magical powers – powers that have been lying dormant for too long.

It's time to embrace the magic of who you really are and invite the fairy mystic within to come alive...

## Exercise: Fairy mystic awakening meditation

Close your eyes and take a deep, deep breath in ... and out... Feel your body relax.

Continue to breathe deeply in and out, and feel yourself sink down, down into the Earth.

In your mind's eye, see a silver cord connecting you to the heavens above as you travel down and down, further and further through the darkness, until you stop in the dark chamber of what appears to be a cave.

You know there is an exit somewhere, but it isn't yet revealing itself. So embrace yourself as you rest in this womb of black velvet, safe in the darkness of the Earth's belly. Become aware of the darkness around you and listen to the heartbeat of the mother, Mother Earth, who nurtures you and tells you it's okay, it's safe here.

Thump. Thump. Thump. Thump. Listen to the beat as it takes you deeper within.

Here in the darkness, you become aware that this is where the magic begins. This is the place where you can really be yourself.

Now, in this safe haven, allow yourself to be who you always knew you were.

Breathe the Earth's healing energy into your heart and allow it to clear away any pain.

As you breathe to the rhythm, feel the Mother's heartbeat, and feel her loving energy releasing any fears, from any lifetime, and lifting them from you completely. Exhale them back to the Mother.

Feel your heart expanding back to its natural loving self.

You see a spark of light glowing in the distance. You go towards it, and as you do, you feel a warmth and find yourself outside in a sacred grove that has been forgotten in the mists of time.

In the middle of the grove you see huge standing stones making up the walls of an ancient burial chamber with a grassy roof on top.

As you stand in this sacred site, you become aware of the energies of many ancient and once honoured deities. You know you have been here many times before and you feel the magic coursing through this place.

Surrounding and protecting the grove stand huge and powerful trees. There are oak, ash, elder, yew, beech, willow, holly, hawthorn, sycamore, elm and many more. You feel the call from one of these 'keepers of wisdom', and walk towards it.

As you stand before it, feel your strong roots attached to the earth below you. Stand firmly in your power and say:

*'Inner fae mystic, I call upon you.*
*Awaken and assist in all that I do.*
*I invoke your magic to connect us as one.*
*By alluring enchantment, united, it's done.'*

Now feel your power rising up. Vital energy surges through you and you feel every part of you come alive as each cell, each vessel and each particle resonates with the healing vibration of magic.

Allow the awakening. Breathe it in. Resonate with the natural gifts of your mystical self. This is a time to receive. Be willing to accept the gifts that are your birthright and fully embrace your natural and very powerful ancient wisdom, knowledge and healing. Be still as they integrate on a full cosmic level.

With a blast of light, a god or goddess of the faekind appears in front of you. You have worked with this deity in many lifetimes and know each other on a deep soul level. Your relationship is as strong as ever; it is only in recent incarnations that you, as the self, has forgotten it.

Allow this fairy king or queen to remind you of it. Take some time to connect, to ask questions, to listen.

Now walk to the burial chamber and through its entrance. Here you find yourself back in the darkness. You see a light shining – the exit has been revealed.

You push through the darkness – push and push. It's a struggle, like a birth. Finally you make it and light shines all around you. You are back in the here and now.

Take a deep breath and allow the silver cord above you to float away as you feel your feet on the floor, reminding you that you are grounded, safe and very much alive.

Welcome back!

## SUMMARY

- Protection is key when we partake in magical work.

- The pentagram represents the four basic elements, as well as the element of Spirit.

- The fairy star has seven points and is used in fairy magic for protection and connection.

- Building a fairy altar creates sacred space for ritual, focus and intent.

- Fairies will slow down their vibration if they want us to see them.

- We can feel the presence of fairies through a change of energy, feelings of bliss or a sudden poke!

- We may catch sight of a fairy out of the corner of our eye, perhaps as a flash of light.

- Imagination is the gateway to Fairyland.

- Always leave the fairies a gift, such as chocolate, honey or mead, in return for their services.

## Chapter 3

# Fairies of Earth

*Shaky foundations will not do.*
*Strength's required to start anew.*
*The element to call is Earth.*
*Connect, restore and then rebirth.*

This element forms the blood and bones of our physical body, so from Earth we come and to Earth we will one day return. When we connect with the physical matter of the Earth we live on, we manifest growth, fertility, grounding and stability. The Earth gives us security, shelter and food – it is our home.

Give yourself some time out to go into nature and allow the Earth to restore you. Draw upon her gifts as you rest and recharge under her protection. Soon you will have the endurance and strength that you require in order to move forward. The Earth is solid and firm, and will give you the grounding that is needed in order to bring about the magical results you desire.

## Earth magic

- *Season:* Winter

- *Direction:* North

- *Magical time:* Midnight

- *Candle colour:* Green, brown or black

- *Elemental:* Gnome

- *Zodiac sign:* Capricorn, Taurus and Virgo

The element of Earth is nurturing, fertile and stable. It is associated with the Goddess of birth, life, death and rebirth, and is fundamental to the magic of spells. It is from this rich element that plants, flowers and trees grow.

The planet Earth nurtures and restores all that reside in and on her. She offers gifts that are steeped in magic and mystery, and provides the very foundations of our life – where we walk, stand and reside.

## Guardians and nature spirits of Earth

The guardians of the element of Earth are the Gnomes, as already mentioned, but there are many other Earth spirits, who are all guardians of their own specific natural wards, including:

- *Dwarves:* Guardians and spirits of rocks, crystals, stones and mountains.

- *Flower fairies:* These tend to their own flower type (*see page 55*) and dress like their wards.

- *Dryads:* Spirits and guardians of their own particular tree (*see page 59*).

- *Pixies:* Wingless, mischievous beings who guide people or lead them astray.

- *Elves:* Beautiful willowy fairies with pointy ears. Excellent at crafts and archery.

- *Satyrs/fawns:* They have the body of a man and the horns and legs of a goat. Protectors of wildlife.

- *Leprechauns:* Irish fairies who are cobblers and bankers to the fairy world.

These all live a parallel existence to humankind, in the magical dimension of Fairyland.

We can work with all the fairies of Earth to enhance strength and durability, crystal, plant and herb knowledge, and security and focus.

## Earth signs

Those born under the astrological Earth signs of Capricorn, Taurus and Virgo are considered to be the most level-headed, logical and grounded of all the signs. Not surprisingly so! These are the grafters, the hardworking ones who see a goal and will not stop until they have reached it – and beyond! Whilst someone born under a sign ruled by the element of Air is whiling away the hours in the depths of their imagination, the Earth sign is usually physically toiling away. Their strength and endurance are to be admired, but they might be wise to take a leaf out of the Air sign's book and rest just once in a while to get out of their logical minds and allow the creative juices to flow.

Earth signs are the doers of the world, though, and naturally enjoy being in the kitchen, working with herbs and potions, and walking out in the countryside. They like to get outside, especially in the garden. Here they feel right at home, creating sacred space for animals, themselves and the fairies to enjoy.

## Creating a fairy garden

All those who have an affinity with the element of Earth love to get their hands dirty, especially in the form of gardening. And anyone with a garden has the opportunity to invite the fairies in!

Of course, wherever there is a flower, blade of grass, a tree or anything growing in the natural world, a fairy exists. However, when there is an abundance of happy fairies working and playing together, a garden will blossom with that extra touch of magic.

## Inviting the fairies in

Having fairy artefacts in your garden is a sure invitation to the fairies, as 'like attracts like' and fairies will always come to see and be near any statues of themselves. This is a good way to encourage them into your back (or front) yard.

When placing ornaments around your garden, always be aware of what each elemental represents. For example, Gnomes, who help to sift the earth, should not be placed on a concrete driveway! Likewise, any mermaid representations should be placed near water features.

Having an embodiment of water in your garden, such as a pond, will encourage more wildlife to pop in and say hello. Don't be surprised if beautifully coloured dragonflies turn up and frogs appear to serenade you with their croaks, for these creatures have strong links with the fairy realm and heal Mother Earth with the sounds and energies they emit.

Fairies will love you for keeping a part of your garden wild, so why not create a 'throw and sow' by allowing an assortment of wild flowers and grasses to grow freely? This will provide a special place for fairies to play in, rest and enjoy. A fair exchange, if you wish to ask them to help your garden become an abundance of blossoming beauty!

## Honouring the elements

Even though a fairy garden is associated with the element of Earth, it is important, when working with nature, to honour all four basic elements of Earth, Air, Fire and Water in some way.

Each element works with a different mood and energy:

- *Earth* creates the energy of stability, support and firm grounding.

- *Air* governs feelings of independence, freedom and vitality.

- *Fire* increases enthusiasm and passion.

- *Water* instils harmony, peace and tranquillity.

If they are balanced, a harmonious space will be created. So you may wish to add the following to your fairy garden:

- Wind chimes for the spirits of the Air to play with. The high-frequency resonance will attract wealth and prosperity, and keep any lower-vibrational energy away.

- A rockery to invite in the Earth energy of dwarves. Also, why not pretty up your garden with some beautiful crystals? Fairies love anything shiny, and because crystals are part of the elemental realm, they will feel quite at home with their natural healing energy.

- A water feature, such as a fountain or pond, will add an element of refreshment and relaxation to your garden.

- A fire pit – a stone or cast-iron fire pit will augment the Fire element.

## Flower fairies

Flowers bring the sacred gifts of colour and fragrance to the world and are a natural source of cosmic energy that we can draw upon. So, whether we are aware of it or not, fairies urge us to literally 'smell the roses'! The natural healing power of the roses will penetrate deep into our heart and open us up to love.

Every flower variety has its own restorative properties, as well as its own fairy! These fairies are responsible for the growth of the flower type to which they are assigned.

Each flower also has a spirit, called a Deva. This is born the moment the seed germinates and stays with the flower throughout its lifecycle.

## Fairy flowers

Specific flowers, such as buddleia, attract butterflies and fairies alike. Wild flowers that are bell-shaped, such as foxgloves and bluebells, work in much the same way. Planting certain flowers will encourage fairies to come in their droves and bring an extra sparkle of magic to your back yard...

- *Bluebell:* The indigo hue attracts fairies. They love to dance on bluebell-carpeted woodland.

- *Buttercup:* The golden cup brings confidence and awareness of your own abilities.

- *Clover:* Three- or four-leaved clover can be carried as a protective charm.

- *Cowslip:* Thought to be a portal into the fairy dimension.

- *Daffodil:* This yellow trumpet ushers in the spring and brings clarity and new beginnings.

- *Daisy:* Holds both the strong male energy of the sun and the soft feminine energy of the moon.

- *Heather:* Perfect for fairies to feed from.

- *Honeysuckle:* Its potent fragrance evokes old memories and buried feelings.

- *Lavender:* Its therapeutic fragrance soothes, cleanses and calms and induces sleep.

- *Marigold:* Connected to the warmth of the sun, it has magical potency at noon.

- *Poppy:* Bringer of dreams and visions, inspiration and creativity – when used carefully.

- *Primrose:* Portal to the fairy realm. Protects the household from harm.

- *Rose:* Bringer of love, healer of the heart and feminine energy.

- *Snapdragon:* Repels negativity and reveals hidden truths.

- *Tulip:* Shaped like a chalice, this 'cup of love' assists with feeling the blessings of nature.

### Gardening tips

Never, ever use chemicals to help grow your plants, for they kill the Deva and strip the healing properties and natural fragrance of the flower, creating artificial lookalikes!

When you call upon the flower fairies to assist in creating your garden, you will find that your flowers bloom naturally, as well as beautifully.

### Exercise: Flower fairy invocation

❖ Hold the head of the flower of your choice in cupped hands. As you gaze into it, say:

> *'I call on the fairies, guardians of flowers,*
> *bestow upon me, your magical powers.*
> *I breathe in the fragrance, filling my heart,*
> *beauty surrounds me, ne'er to depart.*
> *For all that is good, I ask with a kiss,*
> *dear fairies of flowers, please grant me my wish.'*

❖  Now breathe in the fragrance and say:

*'I work this fae magic, with harm to none,
To heal and restore myself – there, it is done.'*

Time for you to bring the beauty and fragrance of flowers into your life! Place them in your home, your work and your garden, and notice how their healing energies, including colour, stimulate your senses on every level.

You may be called to work with flowers, either as a florist, aromatherapist or herbalist, or through studying Bach and other flower remedies. Allow flowers to assist you in restoring balance.

## Fairy herbs

If you don't have a garden, you may wish to make yourself a small herb garden, or grow some herbs in a window box. Choose well, for you may wish to incorporate some of your plants in spell casting or in making flower essences, turning your kitchen into a sacred and magical space.

Here are the magical properties of some common herbs:

* *Basil:* Happiness, love, peace and money.

* *Cloves:* Protection, friendship, luck.

* *Cranberries:* Gratitude and abundance.

- *Ginger:* Healing, power and success.

- *Mint:* Banishment.

- *Rosemary:* Psychic protection, peace of mind. Prevents nightmares.

- *Sage:* Cleansing and purification.

- *Thyme:* Courage, strength and a positive attitude.

## Trees

The standing ones have been with us since our beginning. They are wisdom-keepers – long associated with magical practitioners and the fae, they hold the magical secrets of yesteryear and are extreme sources of power. They also hold and support birds, animals and insects, and are the lungs of the planet. Their exhalation is our inhalation. They are life-sustainers, their spirits are multi-dimensional and they are wonderful gateways to the Otherworld.

If you look carefully at a tree, faces stare back at you from the bark, the leaves or the tree as a whole. When you connect with a dryad, the spirit of a tree, in this way, you are also invoking the Green Man, the spirit of the forest.

I often see faces in the foliage of trees and can sense tree spirits. One day, as I was sitting at the bottom of Glastonbury Tor in Somerset, England, I happened to look over towards a clump of trees. As I focused my gaze, a huge face, made up of green energy, projected out from them towards me and for the very first time I literally came face to face with the masculine spirit of nature, the Green Man himself.

## Trees of power

When I was a little girl, my mother would go to church every Sunday and my father would take me to the 'trees of power'. These were a grove of yew trees in the middle of a farmer's field. They weren't easy to get to, but it was worth the ramble. Their energy was forceful and completely revitalized my senses as I sat back against a strong trunk and meditated with the yew tree energies of renewal and rebirth.

Do you feel that trees talk to you, on some level, as you walk amongst them? Do you speak to them or give them a hug? Those who feel led to walk the fairy path have been chosen as custodians of the Earth and have a responsibility to the tree spirits.

How often have you sat against a tree, closed your eyes and journeyed as you became one with its spirit? To be one with the dryad of a tree awakens the spirit within you. The fairies urge us to get know the trees and to draw from their resources as and when required.

Here are some of their magical properties:

- *Alder:* Resurrection and rebirth.

- *Apple:* Healing, prosperity, love, peace, happiness and youth.

- *Ash:* Healing, protection and sea magic.

- *Birch:* New beginnings and births, fertility, purification, protection and blessings. Represents Air.

- *Cedar:* Purification, prosperity and longevity. Represents Earth, spirituality.

- *Elder:* Healing, love, protection and prosperity. Used to make magic wands.

- *Elm:* Primordial female powers and protection.

- *Fir:* Youth and vitality. Used in prosperity magic.

- *Hawthorn:* Female sexuality, cleansing, marriage, love and protection. Used for magical tools.

- *Hazel:* Fertility, divination, marriage, protection and reconciliation. Used for magic wands.

- *Holly:* Protection.

- *Oak:* Healing, strength, longevity.

- *Olive:* Peace, fruitfulness, security, money, marriage, fidelity.

- *Pine:* Immortality, fertility, health, prosperity. Represents Earth.

- *Rowan:* Protection, healing and strength. Represents Fire.

- *Willow:* Moon and wishing magic, healing, protection, enchantment. Represents Water.

**Tree incantation**

*Standing tall, often ignored,*
*branches cut down, chopped and sawed.*
*But the fae scream out and cry,*
*'Stop your wrath, this tree will die!*
*Time to seek the truth it weaves –*
*magic, wisdom, found in leaves.*
*So heal beneath an oak or yew –*
*its energies will sustain you.'*

## Tree wishes

At sacred sites, such as the stone circles in Avebury, England, or the Hill of Tara in Ireland, stand fairy trees. They are usually of the hawthorn variety, which is known for its qualities as a magical gateway to the Otherworld. Here people make their wishes or put blessings into a favourite and colourful piece of cloth, then tie it to the tree itself. The hawthorn fairies take the wishes and blessings through the portal of the tree to manifest them from Fairyland.

## Mischief

Many Earth elementals are accused of being mischief-makers, for example pixies, who enjoy leading people astray (pixie-led!) or up the fairy garden path! Their behaviour is understandable and not deliberately cruel, for these are the spirits that make nature tick, and after all, nature can be very unpredictable!

Sometimes, though, fairies like to play tricks on us by hiding our personal items. If you would like assistance in finding anything you have lost, you can call upon the Earth elementals to assist you.

### Exercise: Retrieving spell

❖ Light a brown or black candle and face north.

❖ Take a piece of paper and write on it what you are looking for.

❖ Hold the image of the item in your mind as you say the following incantation:

> *'There's something I'm missing I just cannot find.*
> *I picture the item within my clear mind.*
> *Please find and retrieve from the picture you see,*
> *and return it then for safe keeping to me.*
> *I call on the fae of Earth energy,*
> *with harm to none, now so mote it be.'*

❖ Blow out the candle and take the piece of paper, fold it four ways and bury it in the earth.

Your lost item will be returned in an unexpected and magical way.

## House fairies

The element of Earth is associated with the home, and in Scottish Gaelic folklore the brownie is a household elf who tidies the house at night whilst the family are sleeping. However, rewarding the brownie too heavily for his services usually results either in him leaving the house or causing havoc, for example by mischievously breaking dishes, spoiling milk and chasing away cattle or other animals from the property.

So take care, but know that you can call upon a brownie to assist you with security in your home and to work in conjunction with the element of Earth to improve finances.

Earth fairies love to assist us in affairs of prosperity and abundance, usually in exchange for doing something for them. If you would like to call on them, try this prosperity spell:

## Exercise: Prosperity spell

❖ Light a black, brown or green candle and face north.

❖ Hold a coin in your hand and say:

> *'Fae of abundance, I ask for new peace.*
> *From poverty and debt, I wish for release.*
> *Please bring me prosperity and all that I need.*
> *Adorn me with riches and the chance to succeed*
> *in all that I do. I ask you to bless*
> *me and my life with your vast treasure chest.*
> *For all that is good, I ask with a kiss,*
> *dear fairies, my friends,*
> *please grant me my wish.'*

❖ Now bury the coin in the earth (in the garden, a favourite spot or a plant pot), for prosperity to grow in your life.

❖ Now say:

> *'I accept this healing with harm to none.'*

❖ Give heartfelt thanks to the abundance fairy, for it is the proper thing to do. You may wish to offer them a gift, such as a crystal, and then let them fly away.

## Winter

Magically speaking, the element of Earth is connected with the season of winter, a time when nature goes deep within itself to rest and recharge. When we wish to work with Earth, it is important to embrace this season and to understand and connect with the lessons and gifts it has to offer.

Winter is a mystical artist who adorns nature with jewels of sparkling frost and paints the landscape with glistening ice. It is a time when breath becomes visible and trees stand strong, stark and bare. This is a season when mystery hangs in the air as the nights draw in, enveloping the weakened low-slung sun. It is a time of looking deep within, a time of hope and a belief in magic...

## Exercise: Fairy queen of dreams meditation

Facing north at midnight, light a black candle (for the quickest way to travel is by candlelight) and say:

*'Now that winter has arrived,*
*I wish to take a magic ride,*
*to pass a request, a wish, a dream,*
*into the ears of the fairy queen,*
*who rules this season of frost and snow,*
*and so towards the north I go*
*upon the flame that lights the way,*
*assisted by this season's fae.'*

As you gaze into the flame of the candle, feel a sudden warmth wrap around you, as if a magic cloak is being placed on your shoulders.

Take a deep breath in and then blow out the candle. The smoke from the extinguished flame rises, and as you close your eyes, you feel yourself rising, too. Continue to breathe deeply for a few minutes as you are lifted up.

Eventually you feel yourself being gently placed upon the ground. It feels hard and cold and you realize that you have journeyed to the true depths of winter. Trees surround you, standing naked and sparkling white with frost in the bright light of a full moon.

This really is Winter Wonderland as every child imagines it to be. Everywhere is covered in snow, coloured lanterns light the way through the forest and candy canes reach high into the midnight sky. You watch with delight as silvery, almost see-through fairies skate on the ice of a lake.

As you look beyond the branches of the trees, you notice a huge old yew tree standing proudly in the distance. In its trunk is a doorway that seems to be inviting you to step through it.

You trudge with crunching steps through the snow towards the mysterious portal. As you do so, you hear sweet singing echoing all around you:

> *'Fairy folk tiptoe soft
> across the land of snow and frost.'*

You immediately tread more lightly, so as not to offend.

When you reach the tree, you push open the door. It opens easily and you step inside, expecting to stand within the ancient trunk of the yew itself. But to your surprise, you find yourself in a large room made entirely of ice. Your reflection shines back at you from walls that are so clear they look as though they are made of glass.

As you stare at the image before you, a voice demands, 'What do you see? Could it be me?'

You turn around, expecting to find someone there. But all you see is your reflection spinning round in the icy walls that surround you.

Then, as you look back at yourself, you find another person gazing lovingly back at you: a beautiful woman shining so brightly that she dazzles you.

As you stare at her, she says:

*'You have travelled all this way,*
*and so you must now have your say.*
*Tell me of that of which you dream,*
*for I am the winter fairy queen.'*

Speak up and tell her of all that you hope for.

When you have finished, she lifts her sparkling wand and carefully waves it towards you. Tiny silver beads of light cover you entirely. She invites you to breathe them into your very being and says gently:

*'Your wishes told are to me known.*
*Seeds of dreams have now been sown.'*

As you look to her in gratitude, you find your own reflection looking back instead from the icy wall.

Slowly you turn and make your way out of the room and back through the magical doorway and spill out into the snow-laden forest.

A fairy dressed in white fur approaches and hands you a black candle. As soon as it is lit, you experience a lifting sensation and take another magical ride across the dimensions.

When you open your eyes, you find yourself back where you started.

Now you have made your wishes known to the fairy queen of winter, all you have to do is relax, knowing that the dream seeds you have planted will come to fruition at the next turn of the Wheel of the Year.

## Working with the Earth fairies

Earth fairies are happy to share their creations with humankind and look for those with a happy, open heart to assist them in cleaning up and protecting the world of nature.

One of the first things they will do is to set you a task. Usually this is to pick up litter that's been strewn across the countryside. If you walk past an empty drink can or sweet wrapper, for example, and suddenly feel compelled to pick it up, you can be sure that the fairies are testing you. Go for it, pick it up and put it in the nearest bin, because this will build up their trust in you and will be the start of a wonderful new relationship between you. The more you follow their guidance in this way, the more natural it will become. And they will always show their appreciation – just look for the signs!

I once walked across a pathway that had a beautiful lawn to the right of it, along with a bench and some lovely flowerbeds. This small parkland was on the edge of a busy town roundabout, and as I looked down, I noticed broken green glass on the lawn that could be a potential hazard for animals.

I bent down to pick up the pieces and took them to the nearest bin, which was quite a walk away. It took a good 20 minutes to be sure I had retrieved all the glass, though, and during this time I had to endure shouts from passing cars and horns blowing, as if I was doing something quite mad. I just smiled and carried on, without judgement.

Finally I put the last few pieces in the bin. As I turned and looked towards a pretty cherry tree, you can imagine my surprise on seeing a leprechaun materialize right in front of me! He was dressed all in green, including his hat and waistcoat, and was about a metre (3 feet) tall. He gave me a knowing nod and then disappeared just as quickly as he'd arrived. I suddenly realized that he was acknowledging what I had just done.

### Earth needs you!

The Gnomes provide us with a place to call home. Sadly, their job today is a thankless and difficult task. Due to our abuse of the land through industrial farming, including the use of pesticides and other chemicals and the depletion of minerals from the soil, they have to work harder than ever. They need your help!

## Exercise: Assisting the Gnomes

If you feel drawn to help the guardians of Earth, there are many spells that you can use.

❖ Always start by lighting a brown, green or black candle whilst facing north.

❖ Use your imagination to visualize soil that is free of pesticides and chemicals. See it as rich and nourishing. See healthy flowers, plants and trees growing in abundance.

Remember that whatever you imagine takes place immediately in the etheric world. Then eventually, with more focus, it becomes manifest in our physical dimension. So do keep up the good work!

To attune to the beings of Earth, spend time out in the woods and meadows, always asking for permission to enter first, out of respect for the magical beings who live there. Then consciously look to see where the spirits of Earth may need your assistance.

If you don't already recycle at home and at work, look into doing so. Encourage others to do the same. Grow your own vegetables and salads if you can, or buy organic.

Look out for the wild animals of the Earth by putting food out for them. Build shelters for hedgehogs and make sure that the environment around you is 'elemental' friendly. Gnomes are grateful for any assistance you can give.

## SUMMARY

- The Earth is our home and provides security and shelter.

- Gnomes are responsible for nurturing the soil.

- Dwarves, pixies and elves are some of the many Earth fairies.

- Capricorn, Taurus and Virgo are the Earth signs of the zodiac.

- Creating a fairy garden invites in the fairies.

- Flower fairies are assigned to specific flower types.

- Flowers have their own magical properties.

- Trees are guardians of the planet and we can draw on their resources.

- We can be 'pixie-led' by mischievous fairies.

- Earth fairies can retrieve lost items, if requested.

- The season of winter is connected, in magical terms, with the element of Earth.

- We can assist the Earth fairies by recycling, buying organic produce and protecting wildlife.

## Chapter 4

# Fairies of Air

*Air sweeps in with all its might.*
*Clarity gives you sacred sight.*
*Imagination is the key.*
*Unleash your gift, trust what you see.*

Air is our life-sustainer. It is essential for survival. It calls us to breathe deeply and governs both movement and stillness. The power of Air sweeps through our imagination, inspiring us and urging us to believe what we see can become reality. For imagination is the gateway to magic.

The fairies of Air are the magical beings who fuel our imagination. Shapes in the sky, vivid colours as we close our eyes and repetitive signs and symbols are all confirmation of their messages.

Air is the bringer of new life, new possibilities, and is reflected through the four winds that carry our thoughts and dreams, binding them together into one force of visualization and focus. Air blows us in the direction of new beginnings. So throw caution to the wind and trust your visions as they manifest into reality...

## Air magic

- *Season:* Spring
- *Direction:* East
- *Magical time:* Dawn
- *Candle colour:* Yellow
- *Elemental:* Sylph
- *Zodiac sign:* Aquarius, Gemini and Libra

The magic of Air stimulates the power of the mind, enhancing the intellect and bringing about mental clarity. Call upon the spirits of the Air to enhance your creativity and ability to meditate and to stimulate your mind as you light incense and a yellow candle and face the direction of East to greet a new day.

## Sylphs

The guardians of Air are the Sylphs. These are the easiest elementals to connect with. We do this naturally as we breathe in the air that is all around us.

The Sylphs' purpose is to keep the air clean and clear of pollution. In physical form, they are fairies and can easily be seen as tiny pinpricks of light dancing and swirling in the air. They work through the gases and ethers of the Earth and are kindly towards humans, especially those who are drawn to use communication, creativity or the performing arts as part of their life purpose. These people have a great affinity with the Sylphs, for they are the keepers of inspiration and creativity. They also assist us in journeying through meditation and connecting with the astral world.

The Sylphs will awaken any mental abilities and, when asked, assist with creative writing, poetry and even exams. They encourage us to make wishes and to dream big. But they won't let us stop there, for they urge us to take action and pursue our goals, and can help bring about success. They are the ones who make sure that the right doors open at the right time and we meet the people who can help make our dreams happen.

## Exercise: Seeing Sylphs

❖ Look up into the sky.

❖ Focus on the space directly above or in front of you. (You may have to shift your focus slightly by bringing your vision back.) You will see tiny pinpricks of light swirly around. This is the light energy of the Sylphs.

This exercise can be done whenever you can see the sky. I've watched the Sylphs many times from the windows of aeroplanes, as they have been carrying the aircraft through the skies on the molecules of air.

It is a comforting sight, and if you do this, you will find it enhances your connection with and gratitude for the Sylphs. It will help you to remember that they are with us at all times, assisting us.

## Air signs

Those who are born under the astrological Air signs of Aquarius, Gemini and Libra are naturally creative. These are the poets, the writers, the performers and dreamers. Air signs have often been accused of sitting around daydreaming instead of facing reality, and if they could, they would rather stick their nose in a good novel than be out grafting. Those born under Earth signs could teach them a thing or two about that! They would be helpful in assisting the Air signs to become a little more grounded, too.

Air signs love to travel, often can't sit still and enjoy extreme sports, such as skydiving. They love to feel the wind rush through their hair. How many have joined the air force, I wonder?

Other Air signs may find that their relationship with the Sylphs is based on the art of communication. These elementals may inspire them to sing, or play a musical instrument or perhaps make the most of their natural gifts as speakers or teachers.

Whatever your talent or desire, when ruled by the element of Air, you can be sure that it is the Sylphs who are communing with you and inspiring you. Having an affinity with the element of Air also means you love to be out in nature, to be one with the breeze.

This element has the highest vibratory rate, which is why we all feel better after a brisk walk, inhaling a sea breeze or simply sitting outside. Breathing in the air is nourishment for the body and refreshment for the spirit. It can be used, on an etheric level, to 'blow away the cobwebs', meaning that it eliminates any negative aspects that may be weighing on your mind.

## The four winds

Sylphs love movement and are creatures of grace and balance. The winds are their vehicle. But, like the winds themselves, they can be volatile and changeable.

In elemental magic, the four winds come from each of the four cardinal directions and are connected to the four seasons. This combination works together perfectly for spell casting and weather busting:

| Direction | Season | Name | Function | Spells |
|-----------|--------|------|----------|--------|
| North | Winter | Boreas | Icy cold; brings sleet, snow | Banishment, completion, security |
| East | Spring | Eurus | Fresh; brings light rain | Fertility, new beginnings, growth |
| South | Summer | Notus | Warm; brings gentle breezes | Love, passion, relationships |
| West | Autumn | Zephryus | Damp; brings harsh, beating rain | Psychic abilities, dreams, emotions |

## Exercise: The way of the winds

Being able to identify each wind and its direction is a wonderful tool when working with elemental magic. We can use it to work with all the winds and determine the direction we wish the Sylphs to travel in.

❖ All you need to do is have a clear idea of which wind you would like to call upon, then face that direction and blow.

❖ As you do so, you will feel the change in the wind as the Sylphs change direction.

❖ Play and have fun with the Sylphs and be very aware of the wind changes and how they feel.

This is a great way of becoming familiar with the way of the winds. Soon you will be able to instinctively recognize any of the winds the moment you step outside.

One afternoon my attention was caught by a piece of paper that was flying around in the breeze. I was rather concerned, as I don't like trash to litter up the countryside, and so I went to retrieve it as it landed on the ground. As I reached to grab it, the wind picked it up and took it away from me. This game of chase continued for quite a while and I was quite aware of the Sylphs teasing me each time they snatched the paper away. Eventually it landed in its final resting-place. As I picked it up, a shiny jewelled bracelet was revealed lying underneath it on the grass. The Sylphs had brought me to a great reward indeed.

## Exercise: Air magic

The element of Air is a projective energy and can assist in removing negative aspects of your life or promoting your talents. Whatever you want to see happen, the Sylphs will move you in the right direction. They can be invoked through each of the four winds.

Call upon any of the four winds to help you with a situation, according to their purpose:

### Boreas

❖ Stand facing north and say:

> *'Boreas of sleet and snow,*
> *freeze anything that has to go!'*

❖ Breathe deeply in and out as Boreas blows all around you, freezing whatever must be eliminated from your life in order for you to move forward.

### Eurus

❖ Stand facing east and say:

> *'Eurus of spring and showers,*
> *bless me with new fertile powers.'*

❖ Breathe deeply in and out as Eurus sweeps over you, ushering in a fertile time of new beginnings.

### Notus

❖ Stand facing south and say:

> *'Notus of warmth and sun,*
> *bring me love, show me the one.'*

❖ Breathe deeply in and out as Notus gently caresses you, igniting new passion in your relationships.

### Zephyrus
❖ Stand facing west and say:

> *'Zephyrus of fog and rain,*
> *please heal my emotional pain.'*

❖ Breathe deeply in and out as Zephyrus moves through your entire psyche, removing blockages and clearing the way for emotional release.

---

## Feathers

Not only do the Sylphs bring us their messages on the whisper of a breeze, they also bring us signs through the formations of clouds and gifts with the drop of a feather.

Fallen or falling feathers are seen as good omens. They are not only messages from angels, but also from Sylphs – a gift from nature.

### Fairy feather meanings

The fairy pathwalker recognizes that each type of feather has its own spiritual meaning and significance that can be used in their magical work:

- *Condor:* Visions, independence, sensitivity, leadership, death and rebirth, inspiration and creativity.

- *Crow:* Death and rebirth, transition, magic, watchfulness, straight-talking, power and balance of light/dark. Aids the ability to move between worlds.

- *Dove:* Love, kindness and peace.

- *Eagle:* Great strength, courage, leadership and prestige. The eagle is considered a sacred bird and to receive one of its feathers is a great honour.

- *Falcon:* Soul healing, speed and movement.

- *Goose:* Imagination, full potential, loyalty, protection, intuition, bravery, teamwork and fellowship.

- *Hawk:* Guardianship, heightened spirituality, freedom and strength.

- *Owl:* Wisdom, the ability to see situations clearly.

- *Peacock:* Journeying, healing, purity and good luck. Dispelling ignorance or darkness.

- *Raven:* Magic, rebirth, recovery, renewal, reflection. Aids smooth transition.

- *Swan:* Transformation, grace, balance, purity, beauty, elegance and dream interpretation.

- *Turkey:* Abundance, pride, connection with Mother Earth, sharing and fertility.

When a feather arrives unexpectedly on your path, sit with it and mentally ask the spirit of the bird to show you what it represents for you.

### Fairy doctour tip

Sweeping a feather over and through someone's aura bestows upon them the spiritual energies of the bird it came from.

Allow the medicine of feathers to gently sweep your energy field with the qualities you require to fly high.

## Exercise: Feather wish

❖ Go out into nature and find a feather that has naturally fallen.

❖ Stand facing east at dawn, light a yellow candle and say:

*'I make a wish, now cast a spell.*
*Fae magic works so very well.*
*I vow to keep the Threefold Law.*
*Gifts will abound now all the more.*
*This magic is worked, with harm to none.*
*So mote it be – there, it is done.'*

❖ Now infuse your wishes and desires into the feather and throw it towards the east, so that the Sylphs will pick it up and carry it through the air to bring your wishes to fruition.

❖ Blow out the candle and give thanks to the Sylphs by feeding the birds.

## Exercise: Spring Sylph meditation

It is spring! It is time for new beginnings. Find a quiet place to sit, preferably in nature, facing east. Light a yellow candle and take three deep magical breaths in.

As you gaze at the flickering flame, start to increase the power of your breath and become aware of the air that surrounds you.

Feel your heart expand as it fills with the energy of the Sylphs. Breathing it in and out, start to feel your connection with these fairies of Air building up.

As your connection becomes stronger, you start to notice the shapes the Sylphs create in the clouds, as messages, in the hope that someone notices. They blow their messages through the leaves of the trees, too, in the hope that someone will listen, and they work hard to purify the air itself, keeping us alive. Suddenly you realize that Sylphs have been surrounding you all this time.

Now, purposefully direct your breath out before you. Build it up and blow it out and up into the air. In your mind's eye, your breath is a beautiful golden yellow, like the spring daffodils.

As you continue to take deep breaths in and out, watch as the golden yellow breath expands out across the scene in front of you.

Then purposefully breathe more deeply still and send your breath out across the surrounding area. Watch, or feel, as it is joined by a host of Sylphs, who escort this energy of new purity out across the countryside, towns, oceans and the entire world.

Allow the Sylphs to use it to cleanse, clear and heal the air of the planet. As you watch, you hear sweet singing all around you...

*'With all your might, breathe in and blow*
*into the air and watch it flow*
*up above the trees so high,*
*to purify our sacred sky.*
*You've helped, dear one, more than you know.*
*A wish upon you we bestow.'*

As a new magical energy surrounds you, the Sylphs encourage you to grab your dreams and reach for the stars. They are poised to support you, as the heartfelt assistance you have given them shows your positive thoughts and intentions.

Rejoice at the magic you have uncovered through your generosity and efforts. The fairies of the Air encourage you now to delight in the wonder of who you are, reminding you that magic is everywhere and in everything. Go discover it! Enjoy every precious moment, knowing that you are totally blessed and will continue to be so as you assist the world of fae with your own magical touch.

## Working with the Air fairies

If you want to ensure the Sylphs' gifts are given to the world, you should invoke them regularly and incorporate the element of Air into your life. Talk to the Sylphs as you connect with the breeze and listen to the answers that come to you through your thoughts or acknowledge the signs that the Sylphs send to confirm your connection with them, as they did with me one brisk winter's morning.

I was visiting my favourite nature spot on a very sunny but cold, crisp day. There wasn't a cloud in the sky and the lake was frozen. I sat beside it, surrounded by tall stark trees, on a rather frosty wooden bench.

As I basked in the warmth of the winter sun, I closed my eyes and focused on my breathing. I recognized that the breeze was coming from a southerly direction and so I opened my heart chakra to the Sylphs.

In my mind's eye, I saw the fairies of the Air receiving the love that I was sending out when I exhaled. Then, as I inhaled, I imagined breathing their love back in and filling my heart with it. So it continued for quite a while – I breathed my love out to the Sylphs and breathed their love back in.

When I felt ready to open my eyes, I looked up. A small light aircraft had appeared and seemed to be doing acrobatics in the sky directly above me. Within seconds it completely vanished, but left behind a huge white fluffy heart shape, which stood out boldly against the blue of the winter sky.

I gasped as I realized that the Sylphs had sent me a sign to acknowledge that the love between us was very real. I knew instantly that with their love and support, anything was possible.

## Air needs you!

The Sylphs purify the air and so without these fairies we could not exist. They keep us alive. Sadly, they are having to work that much harder as the air is becoming more and more polluted. Before the Industrial Revolution, they had a much easier task, but since then they have had to work tirelessly to clean up pollution from car exhaust and factory fumes, methane gas emissions and even nuclear explosions!

How often have you noticed the activity or purpose of these magical beings? Imagine for a moment the difficulties they must have, fighting daily with man-made pollution across the planet. Time to re-establish your connection and give something back. Time to take responsibility and become a co-guardian of the Air and assist these fairy friends.

## Exercise: Assisting the Sylphs

❖ If you feel called to assist the Sylphs, face east and light a yellow candle.

❖ Then visualize divine white light spreading up through the skies, eliminating smoke, smog and pollution, cleansing and purifying the air.

Remember that whatever we imagine is seen and acted upon in the etheric world, thus can manifest, eventually, in this world.

To attune to the beings of Air, take hilly walks and feel the wind blow through your hair. Sit on the top of a hill and play a wind instrument, such as a flute. Watch the clouds change shape or go feather collecting. Introduce music, dance and song into your life.

If you aren't already, become aware of what is actually being released into the atmosphere. Become conscious of any chemicals that you use that might be harming the air, including the ozone layer, and substitute them with more environmentally friendly products. Encourage others to do the same.

Look after the birds by leaving food out for them. You may feel drawn to supporting a charity, such as a bird rescue sanctuary or the Royal Society for the Protection of Birds (RSPB).

In return, as the Sylphs are drawn to you, you will find that you are healed in many ways and a new world of creativity, opportunity and inspiration opens up for you.

## SUMMARY

- The element of Air brings us clarity and enhances creativity, imagination and the ability to meditate.

- Sylphs are responsible for purifying the air we breathe.

- They can be seen as tiny pinpricks of light in the skies.

- They can enhance our mental abilities, including memory.

- Aquarius, Gemini and Libra are the Air signs of the zodiac.

- The four winds of the four directions are the vehicles upon which the Sylphs travel.

- Feathers are messages from the Sylphs and have special meanings for magical work.

- The season of spring is connected, in magical terms, with the element of Air.

- Connect with Air fairies by singing, dancing, hillwalking and feeding the birds.

## Chapter 5

# Fairies of Fire

*Now call upon the fairies of Fire*
*to invoke new courage and all you desire.*
*Fire's essence will banish fears and plight,*
*igniting passionate flames tonight!*

Fairy pathwalkers have a deep affinity with the element of Fire, for they recognize the power of a flame in fairy spell work and ritual. A flame is the physical representation of Fire and can be seen through the veil between our world and that of the fairies.

## Fire magic

- *Season:* Summer

- *Direction:* South

- *Magical time:* Noon

- *Candle colour:* Red

- *Elemental:* Salamander
- *Zodiac sign:* Aries, Leo and Sagittarius

The magic of Fire brings about lust, passion, attraction, illumination, love, sex, sun, warmth and inner power. Fire is a projective energy and so pushes us to move forward, as well as being protecting and transformative. The motivating force of Fire assists in reigniting the inner flame of passion, fuelling our ability to walk in our true light with full might, vitality and vigour and reclaim our power.

Working with the element of Fire helps us to eliminate negative thinking and behaviour. We can do this through imagining etheric flames raging and consuming any darkness that lies within.

As you invite Fire into your life, allow the strength of its energy to relieve you of any doubts and worries that have darkened your outlook.

## Salamanders

Salamanders are lizard-like in appearance, red, orange and yellow in colour and can be seen in the shapes of flames – no fire can exist without them! They exist in the etheric world until they are summoned to this earthly existence via a matchstick, a lighter or an electrical appliance. I find it absolutely incredible (and love the fact) that fire cannot be felt or seen in this world without being physically created here.

Sometimes you may wonder why a fire will not take or a match will not light. Perhaps you haven't asked the guardians of Fire to be willing and present. They may need gentle coaxing. It is a very sensible thing to honour and appease these keepers of flames. If you want them to appear, or if you would like to be kept safe from the ravaging effects that Fire can sometimes create, then please give the Salamanders the respect they deserve. They are the ones who control Fire, after all! Give them thanks, or a small gift, such as a bright orange carnelian crystal, in appreciation of the light and warmth they bring into this physical realm.

Salamanders are probably the least known of the four elemental guardians, and probably the most feared. This may be due to past-life experiences of death by burning or fear of the effects of Fire itself. But the truth is, each element has its light and shadow side.

As for Salamanders, our ancestors connected well with these magical beings as they gathered together around night-time fires to share stories of their day as well as age-old myths and legends. Incense or herbs would be sprinkled over the fire to honour and thank the spirits who were working hard to keep the flames alive.

Salamanders are also the beings who decide if a volcano sleeps or erupts, and they can strike at any time in the form of lightning. Their electrical counterparts are white, violet and pale blue in colour. Every time we use an electrical appliance, we are communing and working with Salamanders!

## Other Fire fairies

Other Fire elementals include the smaller Fire sprites and the djinn.

The Fire sprites provide the drive behind attraction and desire. They can be called upon to work on awakening the spiritual kundalini energy that often lies dormant within us.

The djinn are Arabian desert fairies. The Qur'an describes these nature spirits as being made of a smokeless and 'scorching fire'. They have the power to travel great distances at record speed, just as one would expect a raging fire to spread! It is said that when the Queen of Sheba made the journey from Africa to Israel to meet the wise King Solomon, she invoked a desert fairy to get her to her destination at top speed.

## Fire signs

Warmth is very important to those who are born under the astrological Fire signs of Aries, Leo and Sagittarius, and they like nothing better than to bathe in the rays of the sun, holiday in hot climates and enjoy spicy foods. They also like to take charge of a situation, or of other people. They like to be the centre of attention and easily take the lead in stage performances, presentations or even dramatic crises! They like to be noticed, and Salamanders assist them in shining brightly.

Fire signs can be accused of being hotheaded. But these are people with great drive and confidence. They may, however, benefit from working with some of the more sensitive elementals – Water signs, for instance. The element of Water will assist a Fire sign if it is necessary for them to look at a situation from another person's point of view or to empathize with someone's feelings.

Elementals will always come to you when you are ready to work with them. Being born under Libra, an Air sign, I always look for fairness and justice, and I like everything to be in harmony. I have always been a dreamer and am a natural singer, writer and performer. However, I used to lack the drive and confidence that the elementals desired me to have in order to be their 'voice'. Then in the dreamtime one night, a bright red and orange Salamander visited me. He sat heavily on my solar plexus and would not budge. The next morning I could still feel him and knew that he would be there until I had embraced, rather than avoided, the element of Fire!

The Fire fairies' first test for me was a sudden overwhelming desire to dye my beautiful long blonde hair bright red! I jumped into it, assuring myself I wouldn't regret it. And I didn't, until the day I was told that I couldn't reverse the process. (This has since been rectified by the elements of Water and Fire!)

With red hair to lead me, I found that my energy started to become stronger. I became more confident and other people reacted differently to me. There was more respect and I found that some even avoided me, for fear I was a fiery hothead! My passion for my work escalated and I was drawn to work with the Salamanders and the element of Fire on a bigger scale.

I soon became absolutely passionate about the Salamanders and they completely seduced me into becoming a firewalk instructor. Firewalking is the act of walking barefoot over a bed of hot coal embers. It is an intense but empowering experience of personal transformation.

I endured the harsh, cold and wet elements of an autumnal Scotland as I sourced logs, built fires and learned the layout of hot coals. On the very last night of my stay, I raked a huge fire and spread out an 8-metre-long (26 feet) path of bright, scorching embers. Under the light of the full moon I stepped onto the hot coals completely 'sky-clad' (naked) and walked towards my destiny, leaving all my doubts and fears behind me.

The following year I met the great Native American Lakota teacher Ed McGaa Eagle Man, who gave me my spirit name of Red Spirit Woman as we worked together in the hot Salamander energy of a sweat lodge.

Salamanders have given me courage and lit up my path of destiny from within, providing me with the strength and passion I need to continue my work, and theirs. May they give you, too, all that you need to move forward.

## Exercise: Salamander fear-releasing ceremony

❖ Take a piece of paper and tear it into small pieces.

❖ Now write a word on each that represents something that you would like to eliminate from your life, such as 'anger', 'jealousy', 'depression', or a situation or person.

❖ Take a red candle and a high-edged bowl and stand facing south (or stand out in nature with the sun above you).

❖ Light the candle, place it safely in front of you and say:

*'Salamanders, I call upon you*
*to eliminate all in my life that's not true.*
*Devour and destroy my guilt, fear and blame,*
*set them alight in your bright solar flame.'*

❖ Now take each piece of paper in turn, bring your focus to the flame of the candle and watch the golden/orangey light flicker on top of the red wax.

❖ Hold the piece of paper safely in the flame as the Salamanders transmute the negativity in your life and transform it through the power of the flame. (Make sure you do this carefully, sensibly and safely.)

❖ Drop any burning remnants into the high-edged bowl, to be extinguished.

❖ When this is done, blow out the candle and say:

> *'By the protection of Salamander fire,*
> *I accept new courage, strength and desire.'*

## Candle magic

People who practise magic have a deep affinity with Salamanders, as they recognize these elemental beings within the flames of the candles they use for spell work. A lit flame can be seen from the spirit world, which is why we light a candle for those who have passed over. Next time you do so, know that your deceased loved ones can actually see it! But we cannot make this connection without the help of the Salamanders.

Candles also illuminate the path of the fae and ignite a spark of inner wisdom. As we gaze into a sacred flame, we know that our soul spark is immortal.

True magic begins with the desire to make something happen. Focus, willpower and visualization are key. Candle magic uses all three. It has been with you since your very first birthday. How many times have you blown out the candles on a cake and made a wish? By doing so you have worked with the three principles of fairy magic that make dreams come true!

Belief in your tools, as well as yourself, is vital when performing any fairy magic ritual. Never doubt the power of your focus, willpower and visualization, for in doing so you are disregarding the powers of the world beyond the seen.

Working with magic is a responsibility, for whatever you wish for will come back to you threefold, often in ways that are unexpected. So always be mindful of the phrase 'Be careful what you wish for'! Working with candles will enhance your magical manifestation abilities, but it is important to keep your thoughts and focus positive.

### Candle invocation
*Magic comes from deep within.*
*Ignite the flame, let it begin.*
*Desires in mind, don't be the fool,*
*focus as you choose your tool.*

You may wish to invite the element of Fire into your home by favouring candlelight over electric light at bath-time or in sacred ceremony.

## Magical meanings of candle colours

Familiarizing yourself with the magical meanings of candle colours will enhance your healing and spell work.

- *White:* Purification, blessings, light, the cosmos.

- *Black:* Elimination, banishment, retribution, north, Earth.

- *Blue:* Peace, harmony, healing, house blessings, curing fevers, reuniting friends.

- *Brown:* Grounding, stabilizing, intuition, balance, connection to Mother Earth.

- *Gold:* Cosmic influences, solar deities, success, wealth, influence.

- *Green:* Fertility, good fortune, generosity, wealth, success, renewal, marriage, healing.

- *Indigo:* Meditation, balancing karma, stopping gossip and enabling astral projection.

- *Magenta:* Rapid change, spiritual healing, exorcism.

- *Orange:* Communication, telepathy, new job, adaptability, luck, control, attraction.

- *Pink:* Romance, affection, love, spiritual awakening, unity.

- *Purple:* Honour, respect, recognition of others.

- *Silver:* Moon magic, protection from entities, inner peace, serenity.

## Exercise: Flame scrying

When we work with a lit flame, we can invoke Salamanders and ask them to assist us in awakening desire in relationships and igniting our sex drive and the natural kundalini energy that is within us.

The Fire fairies also light up our heart chakra so that we may discover wisdom, love and authentic direction in our own life.

❖ Face south and light a pink candle.

❖ Breathe deeply and stare at the flame.

❖ Continue to 'flame gaze' without blinking for as long as possible. Watch as the Salamander within the flame twists and turns. Remember to breathe deeply. Feel a deep peace enter your heart.

❖ Once you feel your heart chakra expand and you can no longer hold off a blink, close your eyes.

❖ You will see an image of the flame in your inner vision. Mentally place it into your heart. Allow it to expand and fill your heart entirely.

❖ Now imagine the flame pushing down through your spine and then rushing back up through your heart and into your crown chakra at the top of your head, awakening your life-force energy and powering up your supernatural abilities.

## Lightning

Lightning is a flash of Salamander physical manifestation. We are warned to stay away from it, to keep indoors for fear of getting struck by it. But lightning is something that has always excited me. The ancients revered its almighty power and I, too, have always had great reverence for it. In childhood, I imagined myself holding up a wand or staff to a lightning bolt and taking the extreme energies for spell work and other manifestation magic.

I wished with all my might to have that experience, to be struck by Salamanders in their mighty manifestation of lightning. Oh the power!

A couple of years ago I plugged my mobile phone charger into the socket as usual. Bang! It was faulty and I was rushed to hospital, having had an electric shock. So I can say from personal experience that the phrase 'Be careful what you wish for' makes complete sense!

In fact a sensible Fire sprite has just reminded me to give a health and safety warning about the dangers of playing with fire! I giggled, but am obliged to obey. So, remember to be careful and to always respect the Salamanders and the element of Fire, and then you will be protected.

## Dragons

Dragons are also associated with the element of Fire, even though there are dragons of other elements, too. These beings of power and might are ancient wisdom-keepers. They can be called upon to bring healing magic into our daily lives and to be our spiritual guides and protectors.

Although dragons are seen these days as mythical creatures, in April 2013 the bones of a 18-metre-long (60 feet) dragon were discovered off the east coast of China's Shandong province in the Yellow Sea. The Chinese have always respected the qualities that dragons have to offer and celebrated and honoured these noble and courageous beings. Sadly, the rest of the world has bought into the myths that have tarnished the dragon's good nature. Throughout our history there have been stories of the brave setting forth on a quest to slay a dangerous dragon, which is always depicted as being full of anger and breathing destructive fire on all who stand in its path. In England, for example, the patron saint is George, who is celebrated every 23 April for slaying a dragon and freeing the people from its tyranny and aggression.

Sadly, tales such as these could not be further from the truth. As with so many stories that are told about beings from the elemental realm, we have been lured away from the hidden reality. This has been done purposefully in order to instil fear into us, so that we may not discover the actual healing properties of these very real creatures. Dragons withdrew from the third-dimensional world a long, long time ago because they could not stand its harsh energies, much like the unicorns did. Fortunately for us, they and their powers are easily accessed in the etheric realm, where they reside with the fairies and other magical beings of light.

Dragons are seen as being predominately of the element of Fire, so will assist in igniting our inner flame of passion, fuelling us to walk in our true light and fulfil our lifetime's purpose with full might, vitality and vigour. But there are also dragons who are linked to the emotional element of Water and the inspirational element of Air, as well as those who serve as guardians of Earth-based spirituality and traditions such as Wiccan, pagan, druidic and shamanic practices.

## Exercise: Dragon magic

❖ If you would like to bring mighty dragon energy into your life, find a quiet place where you won't be disturbed, sit down facing south and light a red candle.

❖ As you gaze into the flame, say:

> *'Dragons of passion, of fire and might,*
> *protect me from harm through each day and night.*
> *Lend me your strength and be with me near,*
> *so I can be free and live without fear.'*

❖ Now blow out the candle and allow the smoke from the extinguished flame to swirl around you.

❖ Feel yourself getting warmer as you sense you are embraced by the vivid colours of red, gold and orange.

❖ In front of you appears a magnificent dragon. Feel its power, feel its force. See it clearly – its colour, its tail, its size, its eyes – for this is your dragon. It is offering itself as your magical protector, your bodyguard. To accept, say:

> *'Gratefully I accept the magic of you,*
> *of protection to assist in all that I do.*
> *Lend me courage and build power in me,*
> *assist my transcendence. So mote it be.'*

❖ Now, as you face your dragon, tell it about everything you would like it to assist you with. Place your wishes at its feet.

❖ As you do this, the dragon breathes on them with the fiercest fiery flame and you watch as they instantly become empowered.

❖ Your dragon looks you in the eye and you see bright love shining there for you.

❖ Another flame is breathed into your base chakra and you feel it expand as the warmth rises up through your body and into your heart. There the flame licks away old hurts and wounds and they are replaced by a sacred glow.

❖ Now take a deep breath in as the glow ignites the dragon Fire energy within you. It rages through every part of your body, purging you of all negative influences. As the Fire grows, it consumes the very essence of any problems or blockages, replacing them with passion and desire and enabling you to stand strong and to move fearlessly towards your dreams and goals with your dragon as your ally.

❖ Give thanks to your dragon and feel its energy whenever you connect with the Fire of the sun, light a flame, feel heat from an oven, fire or electrical appliance, and of course when in meditation and the dreamtime. For your dragon is now with you always – in many forms.

## Exercise: Summer strength meditation

Summer is the season associated with Fire. It is a wonderful time to fill up with the strength of the sun.

Visualize yourself sitting in a special place in your perfect garden. Listen to the birds singing, feel a gentle summer breeze against your face, rejoice at the bright leaves on the trees and sense the life all around you.

Then look up to see a big bubble floating above you. It is shimmering with a beautiful golden colour.

See the big golden bubble float down slowly and gently, down and down, until it stops in front of you. Look inside – there is something inside it. It's a marigold fairy!

She wears bright golds and yellows and is very pretty. She holds a magic wand in her hand and uses it to burst the big golden bubble, which breaks into thousands of tiny golden particles. You suddenly realize that they are seeds, marigold seeds, which are now dispersing over your garden and seeding themselves exactly where they are meant to be.

The noon sun shines down brightly and you bathe in its heat and watch as many marigold fairies sprinkle their magic over their sun-attracting wards.

One marigold fairy hovers in front of you, smiling. Then, flapping her delicate wings, she flies up and round to your ear. She quietly asks, 'What do you wish for and how can I help?'

Take your time and tell her, silently, about any particular assistance you need.

When you have finished sharing your wishes, take note of any words or feelings that come to you.

Then the marigold fairy lifts her dazzling wand. It flashes with sparkly light and she flies to the top of your head and pours a vast waterfall of liquid gold all over you. It's warm and yet refreshing. You are tingling.

Feel this stream of prosperity wash over you, from the top of your head through your hair, over your face, across your shoulders and down to your fingertips. Feel it run down your chest, your back and your entire body, covering every part of you and running all the way down to the soles of your feet, where it forms a pool of rich liquid light.

Breathe in this sparkling array of gold. Breathe it up, up through your feet, your legs and your body to your head. Feel it filling every part of you, every cell, every vessel. Allow it to fill you completely. Drink it in. Witness each cell of your body vibrating with this magical energy of summer prosperity. Let it fill your aura.

Be sure that there will be great positive change in your life now, as you hear the sweet words of the marigold fairy:

> *'Ignite the sun of summer, and know*
> *you are the power, the sacred glow.*
> *Love and passion stirred and invoked,*
> *strength is yours now the fire is stoked.'*

The strength and power of the sun now fuel your inner flame. Your work is done – time to have fun and enjoy the abundance that summer bestows upon you.

Give heartfelt thanks to the marigold fairy, for it is the proper thing to do. You may wish to offer her a gift, perhaps a crystal such as a yellow citrine, before you let her fly away.

## Working with the Fire fairies

The sun is the greatest example of the element of Fire and the impassioned work of the Salamanders. Many ancient cultures worshipped this life-giving entity. The Egyptians saw it as the god Ra, while the ancient Greeks honoured it as their god Helios, the Romans as Apollo and the Celts as Lugh.

Today I am pleased to say that the sun is still honoured. Many of the remaining Native American tribes perform a sun dance each year to honour the sun as the bringer of life, and the Summer Solstice, when the sun is at its strongest, is still a time of great spiritual celebration for many people around the world.

Others worship the sun in different ways, often unwittingly. Outdoor parties, barbecues and sunbathing during the hot and passionate months of summer are all forms of sun worship and an honouring of the Fire fairies who work so hard to ensure we sizzle!

## Fire needs you!

It is so sad that, unlike our ancestors, most people today do not realize that the nature spirits and elements all contribute to the workings of this world. How many people think about giving thanks to the Salamanders each time they heat up the oven, boil a kettle or blow-dry their hair?

To attune to the beings of Fire, invite some warmth into your life. Spice up passion in the bedroom with new red silk bed covers, or decorate the room with pinks, oranges and reds. If you have a fireplace, enjoy a romantic evening in front of a log fire, or have friends round for a bonfire or to chat around a fire pit late into the night.

Sunbathing, holidaying in sunny climates and enjoying beach parties will also fire up your desires, or you may be encouraged to visit a volcano. Within it, Salamanders will dance and bubble, urging each other to leap out, fly through the skies and cover the earth with hot lava. I wonder how many people honour the element of Fire and the elementals that are housed within a volcano when they visit. But, after all, it is the Salamanders who make and control fire itself, so it's always a good idea to have the greatest regard for them and to help them when you can.

## Exercise: Assisting the Salamanders

❖ If you feel called to assist the Salamanders, face south and light a red candle.

❖ Visualize etheric flames purging through a person or a building that needs clearing of heavy energies. Let the Fire lead the way, until the person or place is free from negative thoughts, doubts, fears or the after-effects of an unsavoury deed and is able to 'lighten up' and shine brightly again.

## SUMMARY

- The element of Fire warms our inner and outer worlds.

- Its transformative force ignites love, passion and motivation.

- Salamanders control Fire and appear at the flick of a lighter or the strike of a match.

- Electrical Salamanders are blue, white and purple in colour.

- Djinn are desert fairies who travel at the speed of light.

- Aries, Leo and Sagittarius are the Fire signs of the zodiac.

- Firewalking is an intense but powerful way to move towards your goals.

- A flame can be seen from Fairyland.

- Candle magic enhances magical manifestation abilities.

- Dragons are associated with Fire and can be called upon to protect us.

- The season of summer is connected, in magical terms, with the element of Fire.

- Sunbathing, log fires and spicy foods will connect you to sizzling Salamander energy.

## Chapter 6

# Fairies of Water

*The fairies of Water offer to heal
emotions so strong they hurt to feel.
Cleanse and refresh, connect to the sea,
dive into your heart and swim now you're free.*

The element of Water washes away old hurts, uncovers psychic abilities and nurtures prophetic dreams that are ready to emerge. If your energy is affected by negative thoughts, doubts and worries, by working with Water you can release the emotions that are draining your natural vitality and positivity, develop your intuition and flow naturally with life.

## Water magic

- *Season:* Autumn

- *Direction:* West

- *Magical time:* Dusk

- *Candle colour:* Blue
- *Elemental:* Undine
- *Zodiac sign:* Pisces, Cancer and Scorpio

The magic of Water helps us to achieve balance, harmony, inner peace and tranquillity and to relax and unwind. It is not only connected with physical water, but also with lunar energies, for it is the moon that governs the ebb and flow of the tides.

## Undines

The guardians of Water are the Undines. Undine literally means 'wave' in Greek. These Water spirits are the energy that is present in every drop of water on and within this planet, from lakes, rivers and streams to oceans, wells, puddles and the rain. They are communing with us through every form of water – even in the bath or shower!

Undines themselves come in various forms, such as mer-fairies and Water sprites. These are the guardians of smaller bodies of water, such as lakes, pools, streams and rivers, and the plants and animals within these waters, which they tend and nurture.

There are also Water nymphs, who work to awaken our deepest emotions, stimulating our compassion and intuition.

But the most famous of all the Undines, I'm sure you will agree, are the mermaids. These are the guardians of the seas and are responsible for all that is alive and growing within these huge bodies of water that cover at least two-thirds of our planet.

Selkies are Scottish mermaids who usually take the form of a seal but can shapeshift into a beautiful woman in order to lure a young man to marry them. However, often a selkie will then miss the ocean too much and will eventually leave her husband to return to her natural habitat. I believe that Hans Christian Anderson's Little Mermaid was really a selkie!

## Water signs

Those born under the Water signs of Pisces, Cancer and Scorpio will feel a deep inner call to be near a body of water, and will often be very thirsty! Water signs also tend to have natural empathy and a strong psychic awareness. They are dreamers, often loners, and can sometimes be a bit moody. But these are the people who can see deeply into situations and are more naturally in tune with their intuition, their inner knowing, than the other signs.

Female Water signs are known for oozing sensuality and are naturally able to charm potential lovers. Admirers of all Water signs are often drawn in hook, line and sinker, regardless of the potential danger!

## Sensitivity and emotions

The etheric substance of the spirits of Water is closely related to feelings and emotions. So Water signs may get accused of being overemotional or too sensitive, but the truth is that sensitivity is a beautiful gift. It helps us to be both empathetic and sympathetic. It also opens our heart so that we are more receptive to the voices and messages of the fairies.

What you may wish to ask the Undines for, however, is to assist you in being aware of whose feelings are affecting you. Are they yours or are they those of somebody else? The art is to observe how you are feeling and come to the realization that you are not your feelings. The Undines can help you to understand whatever emotion comes up, and to discover where it has come from and why. You will find that with their help you will soon act and react accordingly, with a more masterful approach.

## The memory of Water

There is scientific evidence, through the work of researchers of the late Masaru Emoto and Jacques Benveniste, that water retains the memory of substances that have been imbued into it and words and emotions that have been directed towards it. Therefore it is important to pray over water, to instil positive energy into it. I draw love hearts, ancient sigils and symbols on my drinking water bottles and the kettle, ensuring that I consume water that is filled only with love and good intentions. In the same way, saints and prophets healed others with water that they had infused with their prayers.

There are many bodies of water all over the world that are used for healing, such as the Chalice Well in Glastonbury, UK, the river Jordan in the Middle East and the spring in the Grotto of Massabielle in the Sanctuary of Our Lady in Lourdes, France. The energy grows within the water and is made stronger each day by the number of visitors who put their prayers and wishes into it, creating an energetic whirlpool of their needs and desires.

Because we humans are at least 75 per cent water, we can naturally tap into the magical properties of Water to help bring about prophetic dreams, enhance our psychic abilities and heal our emotions.

## Mermaids

The ocean has fascinated humankind since ancient times. Greek and Roman myths tell of their gods Poseidon and Neptune ruling the waves, and of sailors sighting beautiful women with a huge fish tail instead of legs.

Tales abound of shipwrecks caused by beautiful mermaid-like women called sirens distracting seafarers with the heavenly sounds of their seductive songs, and of mermaids diving down to uncover lost treasures of the deep. Of course we can use these tales as metaphors to represent hearing the inner call and searching for the riches that lie dormant within us, just waiting to be discovered.

Mermaids are said to cause the sinking of ships and drowning of sailors, but there are also tales of mermaids rescuing people and taking them safely to shore. These tales represent the unpredictable ways of the oceans, of which mermaids, as spirits of Water, are a part.

Fairy pathwalkers find the mermaids' magic deep and nurturing, because of their links with the healing properties of Water. Mermaids remind us to uncover our inner selves, awaken our deepest emotions and feel compassion for those around us.

To connect with the magic of the mermaids we need to raise our energies to their vibration. We can do this through visualization, which is an easy way to access their realm.

So you are invited to dive in and uncover your own hidden treasure...

## Exercise: Connecting with mermaid energies

❖ Take a bowl of water and fill it with shells and blue-green crystals such as aquamarine or turquoise.

- Facing west, sit comfortably with the bowl in front of you.

- Light a blue candle.

- Imagine a fairy star around you.

- Peer into the water and invoke the spirits of Water by saying:

> *'Spirits of Water, I call upon you*
> *to surround and assist me in all I do.*
> *I invoke your magic to connect us as one,*
> *by alluring enchantment we are blessed – it is done.'*

- Blow out the candle and allow the smoke from the extinguished flame to wrap around you.

- Breathe deeply as you harness empowering energy that spreads through you until every cell of your body is vibrating with the magic, beauty and seductive enchantment of the mermaids.

- Now drink a large glass of water, blessing it before you do so by saying:

> *'I drink of this water so it may impart*
> *connection and healing, and open my heart*
> *to connect with the Undines. Welcome unto me*
> *is the power of rivers, of ocean and sea.'*

Now that you have connected with the magic of the mermaids you will become more aware of their energy in the element of Water that you come across each day. Give thanks for the cleansing properties of the waters that we, and our beloved planet, benefit from and depend on for our survival.

## Hair

I can remember being at the local swimming pool as a little girl and pretending to sit on a rock, combing my long blonde hair as a mermaid would do. I would make believe I was swimming with my dolphin friends as I dived in and out of the water, allowing my hair to swirl all around me as I twisted and turned my imaginary mermaid tail.

Mermaids take pride in their appearance and know that their long, flowing tresses represent their untamed sexuality and magical abilities. Hair is seen as extremely powerful in the fairy realm, particularly long hair, which is regarded as a mark of the fae, and is often used in spell work. In times gone by, a lock of hair was used as a keepsake, or as a token of affection when given to a loved one.

Fairy pathwalkers recognize the power of hair and are careful not to let their own fall into the wrong hands, lest unwanted spells are cast upon them. When I comb my hair, I always keep any 'fallout' for the birds, to help insulate their nests, or to offer to the spirits as a token of my appreciation.

For fairies, cutting their hair short is a mark of grief or mourning. I've only ever had short hair twice in my life. Once, when I was ten years old, I asked my mother to chop my long locks into a short crop so that I wouldn't be so hot when we visited the South of France that summer. The other time was when I was 17 and I hacked my long tresses off in favour of a funky bob. After both cuts, I retreated into my proverbial shell, for I lost the confidence long hair gave me and I mourned the part of myself that had been taken away. I felt incomplete, fragmented, and vowed never to betray myself again.

Of course, short hair works well for many people, though, and a pixie cut is always very welcome in the fairy world!

## Mermaid mirror magic

Mirror magic is often a favourite way of connecting with mermaid enchantment and manifesting your desires. The glass itself represents the water and the mirror is considered to be a portal to the astral world.

### Exercise: Mirror magic mermaid connection

To invoke mermaids and their magic through a mirror, first find a hand-held mirror, which you may wish to decorate using shells, netting and crystals.

❖ Light a blue candle and gaze into the mirror as you brush your hair with purposeful strokes and say:

*'Magic mirror, help me see
the truth of whom I long to be.
Unlock my heart – that is the key
to reveal the mermaid. Set me free.'*

❖ Now blow out the candle and leave the mermaids a gift of a blue crystal or shell.

## Exercise: Mirror magic manifestation

❖ As you stare into the mirror, start to ignite your natural manifestation abilities by brushing your hair while stating your intentions and desires. (You can do this either silently or out loud.)

❖ If you wish to attract a relationship, open your mind's eye by seeing all that you wish for in the reflection staring back at you.

❖ If you wish to manifest good health, see yourself as healthy in the mirror and repeat:

> *'I see myself as healed and whole. I see myself as healed and whole.'*

❖ If you would like to attract beauty to and around you, brush your hair and stare into the mirror and affirm:

> *'I am beautiful. I am beautiful.'*

❖ To bring about success, say:

> *'I am successful in all ways. I am successful in all ways.'*

Mirror magic works in conjunction with your own beliefs. The mirror will reflect all that you truly see and believe in, and then that will appear in your life.

## Exercise: Mermaid love spell

Mermaids love to help out with affairs of the heart. They are the elementals of emotions, after all!

❖ If you wish to bring some love and romance into your life, light a blue candle and a pink one and call upon the mermaids as you gaze into your mirror, saying:

> *'Mermaids of romance, bring me the one.*
> *Cast a love spell that can't be undone,*
> *I ask of the mirror, please show me the ways,*
> *an image I see in the glass as I gaze.*
> *I draw the essence full into my heart,*
> *wishing for love that is way off the chart.*
> *Mermaids of romance, I call upon you*
> *to fill me with magic in all that I do.*
> *I see the beauty of oceans abound.*
> *It fills me with awe of the love I have found.'*

❖ Continue to brush your hair as you visualize in the mirror what, or whom, you would like to bring into your heart.

❖ When you've finished, leave an offering, such as a coin, either on your altar or in a body of water, as an exchange of energy.

## Exercise: Bath-time ritual

Swimming is a must for many mermaid enthusiasts, whether they live near the ocean or have a pond in their back yard! However, if you live far from the ocean you may find that bathing is a relaxing substitute. When you take a bath or a shower, you immediately receive the healing and cleansing benefits of Water, both physically and metaphysically.

❖ Remembering that water holds memories, put your wishes, prayers and intentions into the water as it fills the bath.

❖ Sprinkle in sea salts, which will help you to relax whilst you soak and will revive your spirit. Stir them in.

❖ Placing seashells and blue, green and turquoise crystals in and around the tub will help you connect with the energies of the sea and the healing properties of the minerals themselves.

You may wish to light a few candles, too – they will all add to the ambience.

## Autumn

In magical terms, the element of Water is associated with the season of autumn, when nature starts to turn in on itself and we reflect on where we have been and what we have done in the preceding months.

Allow the element of Water to wash over you at this time to bring you harmony, inner peace and tranquillity. Call on the elemental guardians of the west to open your heart and rein in any tendencies towards oversensitivity. Now's the time to connect with the balance of Mabon, the Autumn Equinox, to receive cleansing and healing on all levels.

## Exercise: Autumn magic meditation

Find a quiet spot where you won't be disturbed, light a blue candle and face west.

With your eyes closed, take three deep breaths ... and now let your breath remain deep but steady.

In your mind's eye you are sitting beside a willow tree, next to a pond, in a grassy orchard. Say:

> *'The west brings water, so it may impart*
> *connection and healing to open your heart.*
> *Autumn reflects all that's to reveal.*
> *Cast magic at dusk, for emotions to heal.'*

You peer into the water and gaze at your reflection.

Then you take a moment to check in with any emotions you have. For each one that needs healing, you draw a cupped hand of water to your heart and wash away the pain.

You lean back against the rough bark of the willow tree and feel spongy green moss beneath you. You hear the beautiful song of birds as you sit there basking in the late autumn sunlight that is streaming through the bright green leaves of the tree. Your eyes squint at the brightness, but you cannot take your eyes off this sight – it's like nature's own treasure chest of gold!

You feel warm and comforted and more and more at peace, and you just know that this is the light of the Mother coming to nurture you and to fill you with her goodness.

Soft ripe fruit falls gently from the heavily laden trees that fill the orchard. Nature's gifts are here in abundance, and as the sun moves round slightly the light alters, as does your eyesight, and you suddenly realize that the orchard is filled with fairies, too, busying themselves with tending to the apples, plums, damsons and pears that they have nurtured from their birth.

As you marvel at the wonders of nature and the glorious harvest, some of the fairies turn their focus on you. Suddenly you realize that as you are part of nature, it must be harvest time for you, too. For today is Mabon, the Autumn Equinox, when the hours of night and day are equal.

You close your eyes to check in with yourself. What seeds did you plant in your life this year? Have they come to fruition? What do you need to bring in, or release, in order to move forward?

As you lie there pondering, you hear the sweet voices of the fruit fairies singing to you to instruct you on how to fill your own inner storehouse with all that you need for a fruitful life.

You smile gratefully and promise the fairies, and yourself, that this is exactly what you will do. The fairies dance around you in celebration and chant:

*'The harvest's in, we give great cheer
and thanks for an abundant year,
the Goddess/God now shining through
each one of us, especially you!'*

You join in the party and feast on ripe fruit with your new-found friends.

After a while, you bid them goodbye and thank them for the fun, frolics and fairy wisdom, then step back into your own world, ready to embrace life to the full.

## Working with the Water fairies

Once you have connected with the magic of the Water fairies you will be better able to embrace all the gifts and qualities that they bestow upon you in your everyday life. Be the seductress, the charmer, and allow your inner Goddess energy (men as well as women) to rise up from the depths. Embrace your strength and never apologize for harnessing your true feminine wiles. Call upon the mermaids to assist you in affairs of the heart, enchantment, spells for love, beauty and freedom, prophetic dreams and psychic enhancement.

Once, on a trip to Mallorca, I woke just as the sun was rising and wandered down to the sea. Swimming has always been my favourite activity and I love the beach. That morning I felt guided to explore some rocks that were jutting out at the end of a small boardwalk. I noticed an empty pop can in a rock pool and so I carefully climbed onto the rock and lowered myself gently down to retrieve it.

Suddenly a huge crab sitting beneath the water caught my eye. I also noticed some fishing wire wrapped around the rock. As I pulled the wire, the crab moved upwards. When I let go, the crab fell back into the water. Oh no! It was tied to the fishing wire and was trapped!

I tried and tried to shift the wire, but it was embedded under the rock as well as being wrapped around it. I eventually managed to find a very sharp stone and set to work using it as a saw to cut through the wire. It took a good 20 minutes or so, but finally the crab was released and it scuttled away to its long-awaited freedom.

I rewarded myself with a swim in the shallow part of the sea and then got a lovely surprise: an octopus swam right up to me! It looked up at me with the most adorable eyes, and I'm sure it smiled a thank you to me for saving a brother of the sea before swimming back to the depths of the ocean.

## Water needs you!

The Undines work closely with the Sylphs of the Air when it comes to a wet westerly wind and with the Salamanders of Fire during an electrical storm. But on their own they are continually struggling to keep the oceans free of pollution from oil and diesel spills, plastic and all the other rubbish that is clogging up our seas. They need all the help we can give.

To attune to the elementals of Water, drink plenty of water, always blessing it before you do so. Revive your spirits by soaking in warm sea-salt baths. Splash about in puddles, go dancing in the rain and eat a healthy diet of water-based fruits and veggies, including seaweed! Visit the seaside and take a bag with you to collect any trash that has been dropped or has washed up on the shoreline. And remember to ask permission from the natural inhabitants of the beach if you wish to take a gift for yourself, such as a seashell or pebble.

## Exercise Assisting the Undines

❖ If you feel called to assist the Undines, place a bowl of water in front of you, face west and light a blue candle.

❖ Bring your focus to the golden flame of the candle. See, in your mind's eye, the water in front of you receiving a blast of this high-vibrational healing light and intend this to be given to all the oceans and seas and their inhabitants.

❖ As the light is received, mermaids will offer to take it out to all the waters that cover the globe, healing and regenerating them all.

## SUMMARY

• The element of Water is associated with emotions, sensitivity, prophetic dreams and psychic abilities.

• It brings balance, harmony, inner peace and tranquillity.

• Undines are the elementals of Water. They come in various forms, such as mer-fairies, Water sprites and mermaids.

• Pisces, Cancer and Scorpio are the Water signs of the zodiac.

• It has been scientifically proven that water holds memory.

• Mermaids assist in embracing our inner Goddess.

- Long hair is regarded as a mark of the fae and can be used as a magical tool.

- The glass of a mirror represents a portal to Fairyland when used in mirror magic.

- Sea-salt baths revive the spirit. Add prayers, wishes, crystals and sacred symbols to your bath-time.

- The season of autumn is connected, in magical terms, with the element of Water.

- Bless your water before drinking or bathing in it to attune to the Undines and to help them.

## Chapter 7

# Fairy Dwellings

*Fairies tend to hide away*
*in Fairyland. 'Tis where they play.*
*Fairy rings, crossroads, a mound*
*reveal where fairies can be found.*

The fairy realm is a bubble, a world that exists around us and about us. It is an other-dimensional place where time and travel are not limited – and nor, of course, is magic! It co-exists with our world, but is just slightly out of touch with it, so isn't easy for us to enter – physically, that is!

However, it is multi-dimensional, which means that we are able to visit it through astral travel in the dreamtime, visualization and meditation, and stay connected with the fairies spiritually. It is difficult to see, but if we attune to fairies by acknowledging and connecting with them, evidence of their existence will be presented to us.

Remember that imagination is the key that unlocks the door to Fairyland. It is only a thought away.

## Magical gateways

If you feel drawn to connecting with the fairy world, the fae will check you out first, making sure that your heart is pure and that your intentions are good. Then, as you become more open to the world of magic, they will seek you out. Ancient pathways will show themselves, hidden doorways will be revealed and other portals will open to you, allowing you entry to the fairy realm.

There are many magical places across the world that are ancient portals to the world of fairies. I've been fortunate enough to write these chapters in Glastonbury, in the UK, a place rich in myths and legends of the court of King Arthur and Queen Guinevere, the fairy queen Morgana Le Fey and, of course, the Holy Grail. I love it here. It's a place full of fairies, where you can be whoever you wish to be, for all are welcome and invited to become entwined with the spirits of the land.

The sun is beating down and the Sylphs are dancing lightly on the summer breeze as I look up towards the majestic Glastonbury Tor. This steep hill is probably England's best-known fairy portal. The hidden entrance is said to be part of the caves of the healing White Spring at the foot of the Tor. It is said to lead to Annwn, the name given to Fairyland by the Welsh fairy king Gwynn ap Nudd.

Glastonbury Tor stands on the ancient ley lines of St Michael (aka Archangel Michael) and St Bridget (aka the Triple Goddess, Bridget, Bridie, Brigantia). The tower at the top is dedicated to both, and holds the divine energy of the sacred marriage of male and female. Taking the serpent path up the steep fairy hill to the tower is a challenging rite of passage in itself. But it is a worthwhile journey, enabling us to balance these energies within ourselves and thus be open to our full magical potential. And there's a marvellous view from up there, too!

## Exercise: Tor magic

❖ Wherever you are, to connect with the Tor's fairy healing powers, hold a rose quartz crystal in your left hand to connect with your feminine energy, your heart centre and the divine feminine.

❖ Hold a haematite crystal in your right hand to connect with your masculine energy and Archangel Michael.

❖ Imagine you are standing at the bottom of the Tor.

❖ To invite the magic of Avalon to open your mind and sight to the fairy world, say:

> *'I stand within my sacred space*
> *to harness power from this place.*
> *Sacred marriage is the key.*
> *Fae embraced, help me to see.'*

❖ Imagine you are taking a sip of water from the White Spring and leaving your crystals as an offering to the nature spirits of the land.

---

Of course, whenever we are in harmony with the natural world and are quiet and meditative in nature, doorways can appear through the misty sunlight that beams in between trees, at the change of the seasons or during the solar and cross-quarter festivals, particularly Beltane, Midsummer's Eve and Hallowe'en. Other magical times are dawn, dusk, noon and midnight. This is when the fairy world and our own move closer together and we can more easily see the fairies themselves.

## Fairy rings

Fairy rings are probably the most common form of fairy portal. They are natural rings of flora and fauna in meadows or in open woodland. They are often made of grasses, toadstools and mushrooms, and moss sometimes grows in the in-between places of the magical perimeter.

We are warned never to approach a fairy ring, let alone enter into the circle. Stories abound of those who have entered a fairy ring without permission from the fairies and never returned.

I have come across many a fairy ring and each time have stepped into it and then out again unscathed – perhaps with a slight shift in magical perception and energy, but nevertheless safe. So, don't worry too much – but it is always good manners to seek permission first.

Making your own fairy ring can be a wonderful way to connect with fairies and to enhance your relationship with them. This is a safe way to enter a fairy ring, and the fairies that you will attract won't mind one bit.

## Exercise: Creating a fairy ring

❖ Start by sprinkling dried leaves, dried grasses, ferns and flowers on the ground to make a circle. Stones and crystals can be added, as well as sprigs of a fairy tree, such as holly, hawthorn and yew, and a scattering of acorns.

❖ You may wish to focus on one of the four basic elements, perhaps by adding seashells for Water, for instance. Or you might like to honour them all by adding a representative of each, such as a candle for Fire and an incense stick for Air, along with the shells and all that represents Earth already.

❖ Close your eyes and in your mind's eye see this circle come to life, with mushrooms and toadstools springing up. Grasses and moss grow in between the fungi and tiny little flowers open up. Smell the sweet scent of the grass and flowers mixed with the earthy scent of the mushrooms.

❖ Look around the perimeter of your fairy ring and notice the energy that has grown around it, like a wall of gold spinning around it, creating an energy field that transcends time and space.

◆ Focus on the fairy ring and say:

> *'I create this ring in honour of the fae*
> *and ask for protection on this very day.*
> *I enter this portal, for the veil is thin.*
> *I ask that the fairies welcome me within.'*

◆ Hold the intention that entering the fairy ring is for the highest good and that no harm will come from your visit. Ask where you should enter the circle, use your intuition to listen for an answer and then step carefully into the ring.

◆ Notice the fairy energy and breathe it in. Spend as long as you wish within the ring.

◆ When you feel ready to step out, leave a gift such as a thimble, crystal or chocolate button as a thank you and step back into your own world, bringing with you a new sense of magic and wonder. Your life will never be the same again.

## Fairy revellers

Fairies are known for their partying! People lucky enough to come upon fairy revellers will speak of seeing them feasting and dancing around in circles.

The reason why fairies dance this way is to build the energy of joy that they exude into a 'cone of power'. In other words, all the energy they put into dancing is focused in one direction, which meets in the middle and hey presto – a tremendous amount of magical energy is generated. This is used by the fairies to accelerate their work and help the natural world.

Whenever I run children's fairy parties and workshops, there's always some dancing to be done in a fairy ring. I love watching the children build up their energy and seeing it form in the centre of the circle. Of course, it's a great way to tire them out too, before a party tea!

### Exercise: Fairy circling

*'Let us take you by the hand
and dance with you in Fairyland...'*

So out into nature you go – and dance!

❖ Dance, move and skip round in a large circle. Bounce higher and higher as you feel fairy joy building up within you. Have fun as you see the fairies of plants, trees, flowers and stones all participating until every part of nature has joined in the dance. Dance with all your heart and allow yourself to be completely *free*!

❖ When you have finished, bid goodbye to all those who danced with you and take the power of the fae that you have just summoned back with you.

## Wishing wells

We know from the last chapter that water holds memory and the energy from prayers and wishes that have been directed towards a body of water can form a wonderful elixir of desires and promises. Wishing wells are a good example of this.

A couple of years ago I visited the famous Trevi Fountain in Rome. Above it stands a huge baroque confection of thrashing mer-horses, splashing water and striding Tritons, presided over by a muscular Neptune guarding the clear blue waters of the pool itself. I watched as hundreds of tourists all fought for a position to toss in coins and make a wish, as in the song 'Three Coins in the Fountain'.

This 'magic' is just a form of exchange: an agreement is made with the Water spirits that in return for making the wishes come true they will receive a nice shiny coin – or three!

## Crossroads

Ancient pathways and ridgeways have been followed for thousands of years. Some lead to a definite destination, while others can be uncertain and of great mystery. But where there are paths, there are often crossroads, either where two paths cross and continue in different directions or where one path splits into two.

Crossroads have always been considered magical and sacred places. Nature spirits guard them and it used to be said that you shouldn't linger too long there for fear of meeting a fairy! Of course, that was in the days of superstition and the demonization of the fairy world, but crossroads symbolize meeting places to this day. If you wish to catch sight of a fairy, remember that crossroads are places that join two paths together and therefore where two separate entities have the chance to connect – both human and fairy.

## Mounds and hillforts

*Sidhe* means 'people of the fairy hills' and is the Gaelic name for the fairies in Ireland and the Highlands of Scotland. They are there to this day. Tomnahurich (Hill of the Fairies) in Inverness, for example, is a rather macabre fairy hill, for part of it is a cemetery, but it is teeming with fairies nonetheless.

The *Sidhe* are described as tall, handsome, superbly dressed and fond of indulging in great feasts. Through the ages they have offered protection and healing to humans and even taught some of their skills, such as smithcraft.

In Ireland they are said to be descended from the Tuatha dé Danann, the original minor deities of the land who retreated to a different dimension of space and time when their existence was threatened. They reside in raths, or hillforts, which are ancient dwellings in the form of circular earthen mounds set upon hills. Here they are free from the fear of being cursed, for the Druids placed spells of protection over these dwellings.

They also live under mounds and fairy cairns and in the land of Tír na nÓg, another name for Fairyland, which is believed to lie to the west of Ireland.

It is never wise to disturb a fairy fort, for bad luck is sure to follow. Fairy mounds and trees also are considered under the fairies' protection, and if a mortal destroys or damages these, then a curse is put upon him and his family.

Ireland, along with Iceland, is one of the very few countries in the West that acknowledges and honours fairies. These countries will not allow building or the destruction of nature for industrial 'progress' if it interferes with a magical portal or fairy path.

Finding a magical doorway in a mound or hillfort is quite impossible, unless the fairies wish you to stumble across one. There are tales of people disappearing into a mound and not being seen for many years, sometimes hundreds. When they finally return, after what only seems like a day to them, they aren't quite what they used to be and don't fit comfortably in either world, human or fairy.

*When stars above twinkled their light*
*to guide your way through darkened night,*
*upon a ring of flowers you found*
*an entrance to a fairy mound,*
*and as you bravely took that step,*
*entwined within a world, you wept.*

*Keep the light and shine it bright.*
*Keep the truth with all your might.*
*Keep the light and shine it bright*
*was the wisdom of that night.*

## Stone circles

The mystery and magic of the old ways beckons us through the ancient ones who mark the land, such as the standing stones. These are the wisdom teachers who have stood by silently, witnessing and absorbing every detail of the centuries gone by. They hold the knowledge of the ancients in their genetic coding. So spending time with these gentle giants can unlock the door to the past.

Much mystery and mythology surrounds megalithic sites and there are many aspects still to be discovered beneath the sites themselves. For these ancient stones have been purposefully placed upon natural power points.

Standing stones hold the secrets of the land. They call us to reconnect with the ancient ways of the fae and to walk in harmony and balance with nature. You know deep inside yourself that this nature connection is an aspect of the true you. When you feel that connection, trust that the standing stones are bringing you back to your soul's roots.

Visiting stone circles such as Stonehenge or Avebury, two of my favourite sites, in Wiltshire, England, and the stone rows of Carnac in France is a great way to attune to fairies, spirits of the land and the energy of the Druids, who performed sacred sun ceremonies at such places. So the element of Fire is very much honoured at these spots.

Always remember to ask the guardian of the site to grant you magical access. Then you can tap into the ancient wisdom of the stones and the power held deep in the earth, embedded there by the footsteps of our Neolithic ancestors and the passage of fairies even before then!

## Exercise: Midwinter stone circle meditation

You stare out into the black velvet sky of midwinter and watch the silver stars twinkle. The light of the full moon shines brightly upon the snow-laden ground, which glistens in reply. This is the season when magic reveals itself, and you feel the excitement of the mystery somersault within.

You find yourself at the edge of a forest adorned in jewels of sparkling frost and glistening ice. The trees stand stark and bare, dark silhouettes in the night.

Suddenly you feel a rush, as though something has pushed past you at great speed. You see nothing, but feel a tremendous tingle of magic surge through you. As you breathe in the energy, you look

down and notice a set of small animal footprints in the soft snow.
You are drawn to follow them. You decide to call upon some fairy
protection as you enter the woods, and say:

> *'The forest calls. I shall be bold*
> *and walk through darkness and the cold.*
> *Fairies, I ask of you this night,*
> *protect me from all that could bring fright.'*

As you take brave steps through the darkness, you hear the
crunching of the snow beneath your feet and adjust your eyes until
you see a star sparkling in the distance. You decide to follow it and
make your way through the forest, pushing away branches that
block your path and clambering over bracken bowed down with the
heavy burden of snow. All the while you keep your eyes firmly on the
beautiful star.

Suddenly you find yourself in a clearing and an ancient stone
circle stands before you. You gasp at the sight and feel the strong
authoritative energy of the stones.

As you look towards the star you followed, you realize that it was not
one star, but two, and they appear to be getting closer to you. Why,
they're not stars at all! As you watch, they reveal their true form.
They are eyes, and out steps a creature into the light of the moon. As
black as the midnight sky, with a white spot, like the moon itself, on
its chest, it prowls around a standing stone. It's a cat! A black fairy
cat! You can't believe your eyes, for you always thought the cat *Sidhe*
were just part of the mythology of yesteryear.

A fairy guide appears and you feel safe and warm as she takes
your hand. You move with her, cautiously, towards the centre of the
stone circle. The fairy cat arches her back and you recoil slightly at

the sight of her raised fur. Then you watch, wide-eyed, as shining, gossamer raven-like wings unfurl from between her shoulders.

Suddenly nine tiny tortoiseshell fairy kittens, all with beautiful butterfly wings, appear around her. The brightly coloured fae kitties fly and dance around and sprinkle you with magical sparkles as they mew in riddles and rhyme:

> *'What you expect will not be so!*
> *A fairy cat turns up in snow.*
> *Once revealed, it's time to choose.*
> *New form's a gift – you cannot lose.'*

Slightly puzzled by this message, you try to work out its meaning. Hearing your thoughts, the flying kittens giggle and answer in song:

> *'No need to dissect all that you hear –*
> *a fairy cat will banish fear.*
> *Its gift to you has been well hidden,*
> *but is now presented – the answer's given!'*

Your fairy guide turns to you and explains that a fairy cat will only appear to those who are ready to take the next step towards their destiny. For these cats will cloak you in disguise and enable you to shapeshift into the being whose strength and abilities you require for each step of your journey.

She waves her wand and you shrink to pocket-size and are placed upon the back of the black fairy cat. The raven wings expand and before you know it, you are flying through the diamond-studded black velvet sky.

It's exhilarating to soar over the glistening snowy world below and drink in the magic of the moon while bathing in the restorative feminine energy of the cat. You hear fairy voices singing:

*'Enjoy your flight*
*and become one,*
*this very night,*
*with moon, then sun.'*

Eventually the fairy cat places you back down in the centre of the stone circle and you realize that morning has broken. A cheer goes up as you return to full size and see the first glimmer of the rising sun.

The weak, warm light of the winter sun streams through the stone circle and you bathe in its energy. The strength of the sun, reborn on this very Yule morning, energizes every part of you. You allow it to recalibrate your very essence, to prepare you to become your true self, in every way.

You become aware of soft fur rubbing against your legs and look down to see the fairy cat is there, befriending you. Through her loud purrs, she offers her protection in the form of shapeshifting abilities and a cloak of invisibility for whenever you deem it necessary. All you have to do to call upon her assistance is 'mew'!

You crouch down as the fairy cat allows you to stroke her – a great honour indeed! The fae kittens play around you.

When you are ready to leave, your fairy guide leads you to the edge of the forest, where you make a promise to yourself that you will leave a saucer of milk out in future to thank your feline fairy friends. For at this mystical time of midwinter you have been welcomed into their 'destruction' of wild cats and initiated as an all-powerful *Felis fae*.

## Fairy cats

The Celts thought that cats had a strong sense of knowing, magical powers of divination and their own fairy court. Fairy cats would fight over their hidden treasures and would make agreements to bestow treasures on humans in return for submission to the fairy realm.

Cats were also believed to be the familiar spirits of witches. They would be sent by a fairy court to act as a mediator between that court and the witch. As such, the cat both assisted and controlled the witch, for it was not only its job to help her but also to make sure that she followed the orders of the fairy queen and the sleek black king of cats.

In Breton fairy lore, a person would sometimes make a deal with a cat to make them wealthy in return for serving the fairies, while the Danish tell the tale of a troll who takes the form of a cat in order to hide after he is accused of having an affair with the wife of the king of the trolls.

Across northern Europe the Celts believed that house fairies took the physical form of cats. I sometimes wonder if Puss in Boots was actually a fairy cat!

The very night after I was given the vision of the stone circle fairy cat meditation, something jumped on my bed as I was falling asleep. I froze until I felt padding and pawing and realized that I had brought a fairy cat into my life by focusing on her and giving her energy. Here she was now, settling down for the night. As she curled up on my bed, I made her most welcome. She is now a regular visitor to my bedroom, coming most nights. I haven't told my black cat, Anubis, yet, though!

## SUMMARY

- Fairyland is in a different dimension, but is accessible through portals.

- Fairy rings grow naturally and are made of mushrooms and toadstools.

- Always ask permission before stepping into a fairy ring.

- Throwing coins into a wishing well is a form of exchange with the Water spirits.

- Crossroads are magical meeting places for both humans and fairies.

- The *Sidhe* reside in fairy mounds in the Scottish and Irish hills.

- Stone circles mark the power of sacred ley lines and hold ancient wisdom.

- Fairy cats bestow treasures upon humans in exchange for submission to the fairy realm.

## Chapter 8

# Fairy Glamour

*A royal summons to cavort*
*invites you to the fairy court.*
*Trumpets sound in jubilation,*
*honouring the celebration.*

Once upon a time in an enchanted land far, far away there lived a king and queen...

And they live there still and colour our dreams and spark our creativity by visiting us via our imagination.

It is much easier for fairies to be accepted by us in this way. But don't be fooled into thinking that vivid imagination is all there is to the fairy realm. Believe me when I say fairies do exist! They live in societies, just as we do, and have hierarchies, including a class system!

## Royal courts

'Trooping fairies' are the fairy aristocracy, who are known for their fabulous processions or 'fairy rades'. They live in royal courts that are made up of princes, princesses, lords and ladies and ruled over by a fairy queen and king.

These royal courts are organized much the same way as their human counterparts in the UK, Scandinavia and other parts of Europe. Fairy societies reflect ours. In countries such as the USA and Australia, for example, fairies have adapted their societies to match their host countries' hierarchy and culture.

There are many fairy courts in different locations, including the Seelie and Unseelie Courts of Scotland. Whilst the Seelie Court is friendly, the Unseelie Court is not, and should be avoided. The fairies of this court represent the wilds of the untamed landscape and 'dreich' weather of the highlands and lowlands of bonnie Scotland.

## Fairy queens and fairy kings

The ruler of a fairy court is the fairy queen. The fairy king does not have quite as much gravitas as the queen, for it is the female fae who is the magical personification of Mother Nature.

However, the fairy king will be a great protector of both queen and kingdom. As a fairy pathwalker you, too, will be under his protection. He will ride with you through any personal dark forest to the shining sunlight on the other side.

Fairy queens and kings were all once respected and honoured by humankind. They were our deities, our gods and goddesses, until they were forced into the 'retirement' of myth and legend.

But no matter how far they have been pushed back into history, these royal appointees are still the ruling consciousness of our beloved natural world. They call to us to remind us of who they are and they will always offer us a royal reward when we focus reverent attention on them. Here are some of them:

- *Aine* (Irish): Midsummer queen of love, growth, cattle and light.

- *Arawn* (Welsh): Powerful king of Annwn, the Welsh Fairyland.

- *Arianrhod* (Welsh): Queen of fertility, rebirth and the weaving of cosmic time and fate.

- *Badb* (Irish): A shapeshifting warrior queen of life, death, wisdom and inspiration.

- *Blodeuwedd* (Welsh): Queen of flowers and beauty. Her name means 'Flower Face'.

- *Branwen* (Welsh): Queen of love. Her name means 'Blessed Raven'.

- *Brigid* (Irish): Fairy queen of Ireland, England and Scotland. Her names include Brigantia and Bride.

- *Cailleach Bheur* (Scottish): The hag, the destroyer queen who rules over disease, death, wisdom, seasonal rites and weather magic.

- *Caireen* (Irish): A protective queen and patroness of children.

- *Coventina* (English): Queen of the sacred waters.

- *Danu* (Irish): Fairy queen of the Tuatha dé Danann.

- *Epona* (Irish): Fairy queen of horses and mules.

- *Finvarra* (Irish): Husband of Queen Oonagh (*see below*). Womanizer and lover of mortal women.

- *Flidais* (Irish): Queen of woodland, wild animals and cattle.

- *Gwynn ap Nudd* (Welsh): His betrothal to the fairy Creiddylad celebrates the turn of winter to spring.

- *Mab* (Welsh/English): Powerful queen of all the fairies. Also known as Maeve (Irish).

- *Manannan Mac Lir* (Manx): King of the Irish Sea, the Isle of Man and the Tuatha dé Danann.

- *Midar* (Irish): King of Tuatha dé Danann who loved and lost a mortal queen.

- *Morgan Le Fay* (Welsh/Breton): Queen of Avalon, sea fairy, keeper of the fairy faith.

- *Niamh* (Irish): Queen of Tír na nÓg – 'she of golden hair and shining beauty'.

- *Nimuë* (British): Lady of the Lake of Avalon. Enchantress and captivating.

- *Nuada* (Irish): Warrior king of the Tuatha dé Danann. He lost a hand, but it was replaced by a silver one.

- *Oberon* (Germanic): Married to the fairy queen Titania. Made famous in Shakespeare's *A Midsummer Night's Dream*.

- *Oonagh* (Irish): Queen of beauty and grace. Married to King Finvarra of Ireland.

- *Rhiannon* (Welsh): Celtic queen of the night, fertility, the moon and death.

- *Wayland the Smith* (English Saxon): Elf king and master smith of horses and the full moon.


Fairy queens shine out in their glistening gossamer finery. Each has strong, spirited qualities that we can call on when we need to be strong, feisty and courageous. And yet they also offer beautiful, nurturing, compassionate aspects to guide us through our own phases and changes in life.

A fairy queen teaches us to lead, to unite with others and ourselves and to put in place our own boundaries, so that we can be the ruler of our very own kingdom. She reminds us to be the absolute highest version of ourselves – to be enchanting, desirable and stand in our personal power. We are invited, by royal appointment, to take a leaf out of her book and respect ourselves and the world of nature, and to live life to the full and embrace every experience.

Fairy kings lose none of their masculinity by showing their sensitive side, but they never shy away from bravery, determination and heroics. Whether you are male or female, fairy kings will assist you in tapping into your masculine side, without unnecessary aggression. And every one of us, whether male or female, has an inner fairy queen who helps us connect with the untamed sexuality of glorious femininity.

By calling upon both fairy queen and king, we can address the balance of outer relationships, as well as our relationship with ourselves, thus becoming the magical ruler of our very own kingdom!

### Royal incantation

*Fairy king and fairy queen*
*processions troop through quite unseen.*
*But what calls you, oh child of dawn?*
*One so young, and yet who's sworn*

*by the magical ones to keep a guard*
*on the truth and wonder of the real back yard.*
*Challenge comes, so observe well*
*lessons learned to show and tell.*
*Honour is for what you stand,*
*so make a change across the land.*
*Fairy king and fairy queen,*
*fairy rings and fairies seen,*
*seek their wisdom, 'tis all around.*
*Speak their truth, for magic abounds.*

## Glamour

Whenever a fairy wishes to be seen by humankind, they use fairy magic to slow down their vibration. Sometimes they deliberately enhance their shining beauty to pull us in with all sorts of fairy enchantments, charm and other illusions. This magic is called 'glamour' and isn't real in the world we live in. But fairies use it to shapeshift into animals, to appear shorter or taller than they really are and to appear in human form and as we expect to see them.

The very beautiful wicked queen used a touch of fairy glamour when she appeared as an old crone offering a shiny red apple to a vulnerable and unsuspecting Snow White. This is a perfect example of glamour.

Glamour is something of which our ancestors were all too aware. It was known, for example, that sometimes fairies would need a human midwife and so they would use glamour to disguise themselves as humans, so as not to perturb the visiting woman. But 13th-century writings tell of a fairy ointment that, when rubbed onto human eyes, could shatter a fairy illusion.

In reality, fairy queens and kings are well known for their bewitching sexual magnetism. For the fairy realm is the driving force behind all natural life, which is continually reproducing. So fairies exude sexuality and promiscuity, which they revere as sacred and natural. They naturally pass this potent energy on to us when we come into contact with them, helping us to feel good about ourselves and tap into each turn of the cycle of nature's growth.

Some fairies like to use glamour to create mischief by moving objects or to distract or confuse humans. Don't be fooled if you are pixie led down an unfamiliar path to find a fairy feast waiting for you. Not everything is what it seems when it comes to fairy glamour, and fairy food is not to be trusted in our dimension.

However, there's nothing wrong in working a bit of glamour magic from time to time, and the fairies do love to create! They also understand that we enjoy beauty and like to look our best.

Fairies have their own beauty routine, which is full of magical nature tips and tricks, and they are only too willing to share it with us, if we will but ask. One of my favourite fairy tricks is to splash my face with dew at dawn to make the most of its rejuvenative properties.

## Exercise: Fairy beautiful meditation

If you would like to bring some glamour into your life, find a quiet, comfortable spot preferably next to a plant or somewhere safe in nature.

Allow yourself to relax, close your eyes, take three deep cleansing breaths and when you are ready, say:

> *'Fairies of beauty, please help me to be*
> *dazzling and gorgeous for all of life to see.*
> *Share, if you will, your tricks of the trade,*
> *make me as pretty and perfect as you all are made.'*

Now see yourself sitting in a field next to a crystal blue pool at the magical fairy time of dawn. See the sun starting to rise slowly in the sky. Soak in its nourishing energy as you relax and listen to the birds singing their morning chorus.

As you look over the field you see small shining orbs of light dancing in the distance. As they come nearer, they grow larger and brighter until you can clearly see that they are fairies – beautiful fairies.

These are the fairies of beauty, who have heard your request and have come to assist you.

The fairies take you over to the crystal blue pool and ask you to kneel at the water's edge. The water is so clear that you easily see a reflection staring back at you – but not one that you were expecting. The reflection looks like you except for a few remarkable differences:

your hair is richer, shinier and how you've always desired it to be, your face is smooth and glowing, your eyes sparkle like jewels and your teeth are pearly white. You are a picture of health and dazzling beauty that nearly takes your breath away.

But as you look again, you notice that this isn't all, for protruding from your back are the most ethereal gossamer wings, you are sporting elegant elfin-like ears and you are wearing an outfit made up of delicate petals and fine-spun web.

'This is your natural fairy self,' sing the fae of beauty in unison. 'This is how we see you. Now take a closer look.'

As you peer into the pool, you notice that not only do you look beautiful, but you are also shining from within! You exude confidence, strength, inner power and, of course, beauty. Golden energy swirls and dances around you. So breathe in and bathe in your own radiance.

The fairies of beauty offer you a sip of freshly collected morning dew from the healing sunshine energies of a buttercup. As you drink from this golden cup, feel the very life-force of nature awaken every part of you.

As you assimilate the potent energies, you become one with the gift that Mother Nature is bestowing upon you – your own natural beauty, which has always been there.

When you are ready, thank the beauty fairies for revealing to you the truth of your perfection. Now take a deep breath and open your eyes, beautiful one.

## Love fairies

Fairies are natural manifestors, making anything they desire a reality. We can do the same, too, but the problem with us is that our ego kicks in and we doubt our manifesting ability, either consciously or subconsciously. Fortunately for us, we can call on the fairies to help us to bring about what we really want.

If you would like to bring romance into your life, or to find your true love, then you can call upon the love fairies, who are experts in these matters. These fairies just adore anything to do with affairs of the heart and are more than happy to assist in bringing romance your way. They are equally happy to help bring about self-love and a romance with all of life, if that's what you would like to ask for.

### Exercise: Fairy romance spell

❖ Write a wish list of all the love and romance you desire in your life.

❖ Light a red candle and watch the tiny Fire spirits dance in the flickering flame. Fire is the element that ignites passion, love and attraction and stimulates your ideas and visions in order to bring about the romance your soul yearns for.

❖ As you watch the flickering flame, take three deep breaths.

❖ Now say:

> *'Fairies of romance, bring me the one.*
> *Cast a love spell that can't be undone.*
> *As I light a candle, please show me the ways.*
> *An image I see in the flame as I gaze*
> *and draw on the essence full into my heart,*
> *wishing for love that is way off the chart.'*

❖ Close your eyes and feel, or see in your mind, a beautiful red bubble surrounding you. Feel the warmth from this colour until you feel your heart glow as it expands like a beautiful red rose unfolding its petals.

❖ Now say:

> *'Fairies of love, I call upon you.*
> *Surround me with romance in all that I do.*
> *Desires, now shared, I wish to ignite*
> *my passionate dreams so that I might*
> *attract beauty and love into my world.*
> *May mystery of love right now be unfurled,*
> *to bring me romance, kisses and laughter,*
> *and be in my heart, happily ever after.'*

❖ Suddenly the red bubble bursts and you are showered with hundreds of delicate, heavenly scented red rose petals. As they fall softly all around you, rose flower fairies appear. These are the love fairies you have called on. Take your time to tell them, in detail, your dreams and hopes for love and romance.

❖ A rose red fairy points to the burning flame of the red candle you lit earlier. As you peer into it, you see an image of your true love appear. You watch as a scene plays out of all that you have dreamed of and your wishes come true.

❖ Now wrap this vision in love and hold it in your heart. Feel magic take place as you breathe in the very essence of your true love and experience the harmonious blending of your energies. The love fairies weave around you in a whirlwind of petals and disappear into their realm, for they have work to do to bring about all that they have promised.

❖ Now take your wish list and allow the fire spirits to safely consume it in their flame, dissolving with it any doubts or self-worth issues you may have been holding on to.

❖ You are now free and ready to receive the love and romance that you have desired for so long, for your heart has been ignited! Say:

> *'Dropping within, I now realize*
> *the person I love is wonderfully wise*
> *and has been with me from since time began.*
> *'Tis me, for I've wished for all that I am!'*

## Our fairy godmother

Most of us have wished for a fairy godmother to help us through a difficult time or to grant a wish with the wave of a magic wand. Luckily, this magical being exists!

Our fairy godmother has magical powers and brings good fortune to those who ask for her help. She watches over us from the enchanted fairy realm of the astral plane as she waits to be called upon. She is the Goddess in disguise, and can come in the form of Maiden, Mother or Crone, depending on what is called for.

She has been around since the birth of magic itself and is a force to be reckoned with. She presides over our destiny as she spins her web of fate. She reminds us that lack of belief destroys our inner mystic and power and that the time to reclaim our birthright is now!

In the days when the old ways were honoured, the wise women of a village would take young maidens as their apprentices and teach them how to work with herbs and the magic of nature. Could these women have been looked upon as fairy godmothers by the girls?

Our fairy godmother is wise, but not a soft touch, for she brings with her great lessons and unveils harsh truths so that we can let go of anything or anyone that is holding us back and discover a whole new world of possibilities, freedom and magic.

Once you have called upon her, your life will never be quite the same again. She will bestow on you a sense of self-sufficiency to remind you that whatever you need is never far away. In fact it is always to hand, if you know how to create it. Take the story of Cinderella, for example. In it the fairy godmother waves her wand and transforms the pumpkin into a coach and the rat, mice and lizards into the coachmen who will take Cinderella to the royal ball. All the ingredients were already there – she just had to be inventive!

When your fairy godmother turns up, she will always lend a sympathetic ear, but you can be sure that she will get to the root of the problem and shatter any illusions that have blinded you from the truth. But be strong, be brave and be comforted to know that she only has your highest interest at heart.

She will invite you to peer into the magic mirror, an ancient scrying vehicle in which the past, present and future are revealed, as well as all truths. For magic mirrors do not lie and they do underline the basis of magic – which is that you may not always get the answer that you want! However, in every fairy tale there are battles between good and evil, and your fairy godmother may encourage you to recognize and work with your shadow self. In magic there is a place and a purpose for the dark. Every hero or heroine is required to stumble through the dark forest, blind for a time until they reach the light and their happy ending.

However, many fairy tales present the fairy godmother as a kind fairy who will listen, sympathize and assist in making wishes come true. Think Cinderella's very own fairy godmother and the 'good witch' Glinda from *The Wizard of Oz*. Their loving attributes are based upon the Mother aspect of the Triple Goddess. It is she who will support you in your hour of need, dry your tears and cheer you on as she puts everything into place to make your dreams come true.

Your fairy godmother can assist with all you truly need. So, invite her in and allow her to help you to unlock your true potential...

## Exercise: Invoking your own fairy godmother

❖ Close your eyes and take three deep breaths. Imagine you are sitting in front of an ornate gold mirror at the magical time of dusk.

❖ Peer into the magic mirror and set your intentions by saying:

> *'Mirror, mirror, give me sight.*
> *Show me shadows through the light.*
> *Reveal the one who guards me well,*
> *that we might meet through cast of spell.*
> *Accept, I shall, new power in me.*
> *Mirror, mirror, let me see.'*

❖ Now light a white candle and gaze into the flame. Breathe deeply through your heart centre. Feel the warmth of your heart as it expands into an overwhelming feeling of love. This is the time to call upon your fairy godmother. Gaze into the mirror and watch the flame dancing there. Say:

> *'A magical feeling exists in my heart.*
> *Sacred flame's glow shows me where to start.*
> *I'll look in the mirror, for I'm longing to see*
> *my fairy godmother, who'll appear now to me.'*

❖ The light flickers across the shadows in the glass until it takes shape and transforms into a resplendent fairy godmother – *your* fairy godmother!

❖ She smiles and the love in your heart reaches out to hers. She is indeed beautiful. You notice her dress, her hair and any jewels that she wears, including the powerful crystal wand she holds in her hand. She exudes magic and a power that contains deep and ancient wisdom, whilst overflowing with kindness. Take your time to look at her, to really see her. Feel her warmth and love and remember that on a deep cellular level you know her. Take the time to reconnect with her.

❖ Once you have familiarized yourselves with each other, you hear her sweet words ring through you:

> *'I've watched and loved you from afar*
> *and grant a wish through a fairy star.*
> *A magic outcome favours you,*
> *belief now makes your wish come true.*
> *So close your eyes, count up to three.*
> *I'll wave my wand – now wait and see.'*

❖ This is your opportunity to ask your fairy godmother for any magical assistance you need.

❖ Once you have made your wishes plain, she invites you to peer into the magic mirror. Remember that you may not always get the answer you want!

❖ Whatever you see, your fairy godmother promises you that whenever she turns up she will listen and she will work with you to unearth any hidden emotions that have been festering, such as jealousy and anger. You will have no choice but to learn how to deal with them. But don't be alarmed, for empowerment is her gift. She offers you the chance of new life, new beginnings, through the magical act of transcendence.

❖ Now your fairy godmother lifts her magnificent wand, which flashes with sparkly light, and surrounds you with a ball of iridescent fairy dust. Feel the magic and breathe it in. Allow it to surge through every part of your being. Feel the dream happening – know your wishes are being granted. Magic surrounds you and fills you as you stand strong in your own fully awakened power.

❖ Nod your head and smile to your fairy godmother in acknowledgement and tell yourself that you will leave a small offering for her in return for all that she has done for you.

❖ As you softly blow out the candle flame, you see your fairy godmother disappear from the mirror. But although you can no longer see her, you can feel her presence as magic continues to pulse through you and the warmth in your heart continues to glow.

❖ Now slowly bring yourself back, take a stretch and open your eyes, knowing that you have made a connection with your fairy godmother, who is there for you to call upon through the love in your heart whenever you need her magical assistance.

## SUMMARY

- Royal fairy courts are ruled by a fairy queen and fairy king.

- The Seelie Court of Scotland is friendly, but the Unseelie Court should be avoided.

- Fairy queens and kings, such as Aine, the midsummer queen of love, were once our deities.

- Fairy glamour is fairy magic and illusion.

- Fairies have natural beauty tricks, such as using morning dew as a youth-enhancer.

- Our fairy godmother watches over us from Fairyland.

- We can call upon her to help us transcend our hidden emotions and unlock our true potential.

## Chapter 9

# Fairy Moon Magic

*Mystical moon of beauty and light,*
*may your deep enchantment open my sight.*
*I call upon moonbeams to show me the way,*
*reflecting the magical path of the fae.*

The moon has always fascinated humankind and yet still remains a mystery to us. Its soft, pale light seems to contain a magic all of its own, yet is something that we all wish to share in. The moon has a place in our hearts, as it did in the hearts of our ancestors. Its luminosity hints at our celestial origins. How do you feel when you imagine bathing at the magical time of midnight in a natural pool in a forest glade under the milky light of the moon? Perhaps it opens up a faint memory, a recollection of ancient times.

Today we don't take into account the full powers of the moon and how they affect us every day. The moon really does affect our moods. When it is waning, we begin to withdraw, and when it is waxing, we find that we are much more outgoing. Stories of men turning into wild beasts at full moon, raising merry hell, may sound extreme, but there are many truths in old legends. Do you know that police reports confirm that there are many more arrests for aggressive and outrageous behaviour around the full moon?!

## Spell casting

The spiritual Law of Analogy teaches us that all things in life are interconnected, and the frequencies emanating from the moon affect our emotions and desires, which may be hidden from us. Therefore, the moon plays a very profound role when it comes to spell casting, for it rules the subconscious mind.

When we cast fairy spells, we work with the subconscious mind, the elements and the elementals. Therefore we can enhance the power of our spells by becoming acquainted with the phases of the moon and utilizing its transformational powers. The full moon, for example, is a powerful time – a time to attract love, abundance, creativity and positive energy.

The ancients considered the moon to be the 'mother of witchcraft'. Each phase represented an aspect of the Triple Goddess:

| Phase | Goddess | Spells |
|-------|---------|--------|
| New moon | Maiden | New projects, new beginnings, faith, hope, optimism |
| Waxing moon | Maiden/Mother | Growth, fertility, positive transformation |
| Full moon | Mother | Manifesting desires, achievement, abundance |
| Waning moon | Mother/Crone | Releasing, letting go, shedding, clearing |
| Dark moon | Crone | Banishment, deep wisdom, divination, completion |

## Full moon manifestation

Fairies are wonderful at bringing about all they desire. We can do the same during the full moon, for this is when magic abounds. At this time, magical energy runs through everything we focus on and our manifestation abilities are heightened.

### Exercise: Full moon manifestation spell

Be completely clear about what you are wishing for and remember to take into consideration any consequences that may affect any living thing.

❖ Light a white candle, hold a clear quartz crystal and face the full moon. Imagine you are standing within a fairy star for protection.

❖ Now say:

> *'Fairies of magic, Mother of moon,*
> *I ask that my wishes will come about soon.*
> *Desires now placed in the crystal so clear,*
> *intentions now set, as I release fear.*
> *Fairies of Earth, I stand my ground,*
> *fairies of Air, sweep all around,*
> *fairies of Fire, shine brightly within,*
> *fairies of Water, gift me discipline.'*

❖ Now place your intentions into the crystal and leave it under the full moon to charge and work with the moon's magical properties in order to manifest your desires.

❖ Blow the candle out and say:

> *'This moon phasing spell is now made and done,*
> *with thanks to the fairies and with harm to none.'*

## Moonlight

The sun is our life-giver – we need its vital energy to keep us and this planet alive. When its beams bounce off the moon at night-time, we receive the feminine side of its energy. As the sunlight mixes with the soft, nurturing properties of the moon, it produces magical crystalline energy and rays of light that open our hearts and our spiritual sight.

## Moon bathing

Many people enjoy healing under the sun as they worship its strength in the form of sunbathing. But how many of us moon bathe?

Moon bathing is vital for our balance and our health. We are made up of the same vital minerals as the surface of the moon and sometimes we just don't have enough of them in us, especially in this day and age when so many nutrients are stripped from our diet thanks to intensive farming. So it's extremely important to top up.

Supplements can be purchased from a health shop, of course, and will provide essential minerals and vitamins if we choose carefully. However, on a metaphysical level, the moon has always been seen as the keeper of magic, mystery and divine feminine energies. So moon bathing is a safe way to receive all the nourishment that we require from the sun but in a more gentle way, and with the added benefits of the moon's magical offerings of intuition and wisdom.

You can choose to bathe under a particular moon phase according to your needs (*see table on page 167*). Alternatively, the full moon is when the moon's magic is at its optimum and bathing under it will charge you up with its natural powers. It will also do the same for your crystals – why not leave them on a window sill under the full moon's gaze for a supercharge of empowerment?

## Exercise: Moon-bathing ceremony

❖ Step outside sky-clad in honour of the Triple Goddess who watches over you, or, if you prefer to preserve your modesty, wear underwear or swimwear. Stand with arms outstretched to the moon and say:

> *'I call you down this very night*
> *to shower within your divine light.*
> *Replenish me, cleanse me deep inside,*
> *For 'tis where magic doth reside.'*

❖ Breathe deeply and allow yourself to soak up the moon's magic.

❖ Bathe in this way for as long as feels necessary and comfortable.

❖ Then, before you move back indoors, say:

> *'This healing is worked, with harm to none.*
> *So mote it be – there, it is done.'*

Never forget that the energy of the moon also lives within you as you work in conjunction with her phases, honouring the new, full and dark aspects of Maiden, Mother and Crone.

## Fairy moon farming

Ancient civilizations used the moon to scry with and to predict weather patterns. They also noticed how nature was affected by the moon cycles, from the tides of the oceans to the emotions and behaviour of people and animals.

Farmers have always planted according to the moon cycles and in conjunction with the movement of the planets. They have understood that each of the phases of the moon influences the way vegetation grows on the planet through the rising and falling of the moisture in the ground and in the plants. The new moon is an excellent time to sow leafy plants like cabbages, broccoli and cauliflower, for instance.

Certain crops also fare better when planted whilst the moon is in a specific constellation. As the moon can pass through a constellation in only two to three days, it was vital to adhere to the planting calendar.

But it's not just planting that is the most important time for the farmer, for harvest time also has to be considered. Harvesting at the correct time ensures crops last much longer. It is down to how the plant stores the water in the fruit/crop at different times of the moon cycle.

Most farmers still work according to the farming 'almanac'. But do they really know why? Do the farmers of today actually realize they are following the old ways of fairy moon magic?!

## Fairy moon plants

Plants are teachers. Each and every plant has its own medicine, or properties, to offer all of life on this planet.

Many shamans use hallucinogenic plants to 'travel within' to the Otherworld to connect with spirits. They pray with the 'medicine' beforehand and then take a journey of the mind to discover what it is they need to know for healing and other magical purposes. But actually fairies teach us that we can learn from any plant, not just from hallucinogenics (as long as the plant isn't poisonous to ingest of course), and we can connect with the energies of the moon, too, through certain flowers and herbs.

- *Belladonna:* This was ingested by the priests of the goddess Bellona prior to worshipping her. This is not recommended, as belladonna is not only psychotropic, but also poisonous! Get the measurement right and it will take you temporarily into the spirit world, but please do not ingest it! To work with it safely, use an incense blend and burn it under a new moon to manifest your desires.

- *Daisy (day's eye):* This flower holds the energy of the sun in its yellow centre and that of the moon in its white petals. It follows the cycle of the sun through the day, folding its petals when the sun goes down and the moon ascends. Ingesting a daisy is completely safe and connects you to the frequency of both sun and moon, thus balancing the male and female energies within.

- *Mugwort:* This vibrates at the same frequency as the moon, so can be used to connect with the energies of the moon, even when it's not visible. Adding mugwort to a pot of tea is completely safe and infuses your entire body with moon magic!

- *Rose:* The flower of Aphrodite, the goddess of love. Did you ever collect rose petals as a child and make perfumed rose water? Roses hold the love vibration of the divine feminine, just like the moon. Their heady perfume was often used to send lovers into a delirium.

## Fairies and the moon

Fairies act as the facilitators of the moon's energies. They work in conjunction with them according to their own basic element function.

### Earth

Without getting all scientific, the moon's surface is a mass of minerals, including crystals. Their energy resonates with Earth energy, and as the sun reflects off the crystalline Earth energy of the moon, it beams down to our planet, thus creating nurturing frequencies that the elementals of Earth use for the growth and cultivation of all plants.

### Air

The moon affects the pull of the winds, depending on its phase. When it is in its waning phase, for example, it becomes windier on Earth. When it starts to wax, the winds settle down.

### Fire

The fire of the sun is reflected by the moon so that Earth receives its properties of strength, passion and desire, but in a gentler form, though the element of Fire.

### Water

The moon's gravitational pull affects the ebb and flow of the tides, and we, too, are affected by it, as we are made up of at least 75 per cent water. A woman's monthly fertility cycle is affected by it, for example. Which is why it is often referred to as her 'moon time'!

## Working fairy moon magic

By connecting with the fairies and the elements they work with, we can use the frequencies emanating from the moon to perform fairy moon magic. In conjunction with the right moon phase, of course:

- *New moon:* a fertile time for new beginnings, which will come to fruition as the moon waxes to full

- *Full moon:* a very good time for bringing about what we desire

- *Dark moon:* used for banishing and getting rid of what does not serve

If you feel you would like to truly step onto a path of enlightenment, the moon will guide the way. Allow the fae to sprinkle you with magic as you, and they, work in conjunction with the moon on this fine night...

## Exercise: Fairy moon magic meditation

As the sun starts to descend below the skyline, you make your way towards a grove of trees silhouetted on the top of a hill. It is the magical time of dusk and as you enter the ancient grove, you notice the presence of fairy energy.

You sit with your back against a tree and imagine strong roots growing from the soles of your feet down into the ground, reaching deep, deep down into the earth and wrapping around a huge crystal at the centre of the Earth, grounding you, protecting you and connecting you to Mother Earth.

Breathe up the crystalline energy, breathe up the Earth magic. Feel it filling every cell, every vessel, until you glow. Allow yourself to be part of the evening's magic. Breathe it in.

As you look around you, you notice a circle of mushrooms and toadstools in the centre of the ancient grove. Smell the earthy scent of the fungi mixing with the sweet aroma of the soft grass and moss that lie before you like a lush green healing blanket.

Wishing to enter the magical circle, you hold the intention that this is for the highest good and that no harm will come from your visit. Ask where you should stand within the circle and listen, using your intuition, for the answer. Then step carefully into the ring, saying:

*'I call on moon magic this very eve,*
*when mystique and mystery together do weave.*
*May power be granted this very night,*

*as I share my new gifts, for 'tis only right.*
*With arms outstretched to the magical ones,*
*I give honour and thanks, and now it is done.'*

As you stand strong in the centre of the fairy ring with your arms outstretched, your face is flooded with a soft glow of moonlight from above. Bathe in its soft, gentle energy and immerse yourself in the divine feminine. Feel your heart chakra opening up like a beautiful rose and any old habits, fears, thought patterns and behaviour that have been preventing you from moving forward gently dissolving.

You are being given the gift of receptivity. This is the fae's opportunity to help make your dreams come true, and you hear sweet singing in the air around you:

*'Drink of the moon on this fine night*
*with loving heart and open sight.*
*Show us your visions in your mind,*
*we will return your wishes in kind.'*

As the moon streams its sacred light through your third eye, at the centre of your forehead, picture clearly all that you would like to see happen.

You begin to feel energy building around the perimeter of the ring and notice a force-field of silver spinning around the circle. Stand strong within this fairy and moon enchantment and let the magical workings unfold.

Listen to what the fairies have to say, as they may give you advice or instructions. Allow them to grant your wishes in their own unique way.

Some fairy folk approach you, carrying a beautiful goblet which bears the moon's image. They tell you that this is in honour of the moon goddess.

They offer you the goblet. It is filled with liquid moonlight. You may take it, and as you sip its qualities of intuition, integrity, peace, love, compassion, femininity, receptivity, confidence and higher abilities, they pour into you.

Hand the goblet back and take a moment as the energies you have just consumed are assimilated into your essence. Hear the fairies singing:

> *'Go forth and be the real "you".*
> *Upon the dawn may dreams come true.'*

Feeling more energized and connected than you have ever done before, you reach into your pocket. You have a gift that you offer as a thank you to all who have welcomed you and helped you here today in the fairy ring.

A daisy is offered to you and you eat it. As you do so, you feel the golden masculine energy of the sun and the pure white feminine energy of the moon being blended and received into your body. You feel every cell awaken and assimilate this powerful medicine of the fae and the planets. You feel yourself become one with them.

Fully charged, you bid the fairies goodbye and step carefully out of the circle and back into your own world, bringing with you a new sense of magic and wonder.

## SUMMARY

- The moon rules the subconscious mind and its phases assist in spell casting.

- During specific moon phases, its transformational powers can be utilized for magic.

- Each moon phase has a specific magical meaning, as well as Goddess energy.

- Moonlight is the reflected light of the sun mixed with crystalline moon energy.

- Moon bathing is vital to top up on nutrients and magic.

- Farmers follow an ancient agricultural moon calendar.

- Earth fairies assist in the cultivation of plants under the moon's energy.

- The moon's phases affect the pull of the winds.

- The ebb and flow of the water on this planet is governed by the moon.

- The new moon is associated with new beginnings.

- The full moon helps with manifesting goals.

- The dark moon can be used for banishing.

## Chapter 10

# Fairy Healing

*A broken heart, flu or a bad knee*
*require the utmost sympathy.*
*The fairies ask you not to squeal,*
*for their mission is to heal.*

In ancient times it was understood that harming nature in any way would affect the fairies. This led to the fearful belief that they would then 'borrow' energy from people in order to complete their tasks or even strike them down with 'fairy sickness'. The Anglo-Saxons, for example, thought that some diseases were spread by elves and so a patient was often diagnosed as being as 'elf-shot'. In those superstitious days it was believed that fairies could cause all sorts of ailments and so people sought to appease them.

Today, as ever, fairies work tirelessly to keep nature in balance, and when pollution disturbs its delicate equilibrium, they work twice as hard to make repairs. They aren't helped by the lack of belief so prevalent today. If everybody around the world believed in fairies, then the vital energy that they need to assist nature would flow abundantly.

## Fairy doctouring

Over the centuries, fairies have shared knowledge of healing herbs, cures and ointments with those who have visited their world. Often it has happened during a high fever or near-death experience. On their return to this world, or recovery, the person has found they have gained supernatural abilities and healing powers. They have become a fairy doctour.

Fairy doctouring is an ancient healing system where the practitioner works with the faeries to cure ailments. They take a journey, usually through meditation, into the faery realm to diagnose an illness and to find a cure. Charms, herbs, chants, healing stones and crystals are the tools of the trade. The fairies willingly share their knowledge. Their only stipulation is that the fairy doctour is forbidden to share the secrets of their gift until they are on their deathbed; only then can they pass on the knowledge to their firstborn.

In return for the services of a fairy doctour, no money must be exchanged. Instead the doctour will accept payment in kind and welcome offerings of food, drink or a small, shiny gift.

## Fairy healing

Fortunately we don't have to suffer anything nasty in order to practise fairy healing ourselves. We can connect to the natural healing energy of the fae by connecting with the fairy world itself.

Fairy healing is tied to ancient tradition and ritual, but its methods are still effective today. It is rooted in the ways of Mother Earth and our natural state of wholeness. When a mermaid showed me, during a healing session, that they saw everything as healed and whole, I immediately adopted that technique. Seeing a patient as already healed enables the magic of the universe to deliver that result. Of course a big dose of fairy faith is needed, but when you have fairy magic in your heart, trust comes easily enough.

Fairy healing is a unique path that allows the practitioner to find ways to connect body and mind to spirit, and then connect that unified spirit to nature. We all know that nature in itself is healing. Whenever we go outside and smell the fresh air, hug a tree or sniff a flower, we benefit from the healing properties of the natural world. So when we are performing any fairy healing, we incorporate the energy of the four basic elements and the loving teachings and guidance of the elemental spirits of nature. It is important to listen and 'feel' for the elements that wish to be called upon and to follow their advice.

The colour green is associated with healing – it is the colour of nature, after all, and the auric colour of Archangel Raphael, who is the healing angel of all angels! So you can imagine my surprise when I called for some healing assistance one night and found myself suddenly wrapped in an iridescent blanket of *bright electric blue*. It was my first encounter with healing fairies and I realized their colour was deep and intense, matching their restorative powers.

## Exercise: Fairy healing meditation

Fairies are natural healers and know how to instantly relieve pain and cure dis-ease. Whenever you are feeling under the weather or are afflicted by pain, you can call upon them to help you heal.

All you need to do is lie in a comfortable position, preferably at night-time, so that the healing fairies can continue to work with you as you sleep.

Feeling relaxed, take a deep breath in and then slowly release it. Breathe in ... and out ... and take another deep breath in ... and release it.

See yourself fully protected within the seven points of a fairy star and say:

> *'Fairies, I call on you to come and heal my pain*
> *with your powerful magic. I ask not in vain.*
> *Bring me cures of deep colour and bright starlight made,*
> *And let the discomfort and illness all now fade.'*

With your eyes still shut, see in your mind hundreds of fairies, all glowing the brightest electric blue. As you take a deep breath in, these remarkable healers come together to form an iridescent blanket of sapphire.

This magical jewelled cloak wraps around your body causing a surge of warm healing energy to pulse through you, filling every vessel, every artery, every part of your being. You are filled with perfect love, healing and strength as the fairies touch your heart with their magic.

Breathe in the healing energy. Feel it. Breathe in the healing light. Stay in the moment – rest and allow, as vitality and wholeness are restored.

Don't forget to thank the healing faeries wholeheartedly when you wake and leave them a small plate of bread and honey in grateful payment.

## Crystal healing

Fairies are naturally attracted to the shining world of crystals – and why not? Rocks, stones and crystals are members of the fairy realm, after all! The fairy pathwalker understands that all of nature is alive, that all beings have spirit, and that these conscious semi-precious gems are happy to assist us with healing, connection work and any form of protection.

Crystals truly wish to partner us. They even choose us! Whether you feel drawn to work with them on a professional healing basis with clients or purely for your own benefit, know that they have the power to entrance, enhance, strengthen and energize, and they will remind you to connect with them on a regular basis.

Every crystal is packed with healing energy of one kind or another, and crystals are easily programmed, purely with intention, as they are great memory-holders – particularly the quartz family!

Crystalline energy amplifies our healing abilities, as well as assisting in a greater connection to the fairy realm. Through working with crystals, you will find that you will become stronger and your skills will be amplified. Invite them into your everyday life by wearing them on your person, placing them around your environment or using them for deep meditation.

### Crystal incantation

*To amplify, we should unite.*
*Crystals help to shine our light.*
*Used in healing or in spell,*
*we'll support you very well.*
*Upon your heart, rose quartz for love.*
*Fae gifts from the Earth and the stars above.*

## Crystal shapes

Many different shapes of crystal can help the fairy healer in their work:

- *Clusters:* Transform negative energy into positive.

- *Points* (natural or handcrafted): When they are pointed towards the body, energy is channelled in. When they are pointed away, energy is drawn out. They are excellent for constructing crystal grids for healing, clearing and protection.

- *Pyramids:* Artificially made, these are used to draw energy upwards.

- *Slices:* Reveal the beauty of the stone. Ideal aids for meditation, for raising the energy of a room or for physical healing.

- *Spheres:* These emit a constant circle of energy. They can be used as room energizers.

- *Tumbled:* Rough or polished stones in their natural state. Perfect for using in healing, and for carrying on your person for healing, connection and protection, depending on each crystal's energetic property.

- *Wands* (natural or handcrafted): Excellent healing tools. Energy is focused through the tip.

## Crystal types

Each type of crystal has its own individual healing benefits. Black obsidian, black tourmaline, haematite and smoky quartz are all good protective stones; for example, for rooms, when healing someone or for personal use. They have the ability to absorb negativity and give out pure, clean energy.

Here are a few more examples:

- *Amethyst:* assists with developing spirituality and overcoming addictions

- *Citrine:* known as the 'merchant stone'; keep it in your purse/wallet to attract wealth

- *Fluorite:* provides a protective shield from harmful electromagnetic radiation

- *Malachite:* helps strengthen and heal the heart

- *Rose quartz:* the love stone to bring about romance

### Crystal cleansing

Before we use crystals, it is vitally important to make sure they are cleansed. This is so that we don't pick up on any energies that they may have absorbed from someone or somewhere else.

As crystals are members of the fairy realm, it is beneficial to honour this by using one of the four basic elements to help with the cleansing. Choose whichever you feel most aligned with, or one that suits the particular healing you are about to do.

- *Element of Earth:* Bury your crystals in the earth of your back yard or in a plant pot.

- *Element of Air:* Sweep a lit stick of incense over the crystals. Ring a bell or chime Tibetan bells.

- *Element of Fire:* Pass your crystals quickly and safely through a candle flame.

- *Element of Water:* Cleanse your crystals in a bowl of water (unless they are selenite, which will dissolve!)

- *Full moon:* Charge your crystals in its energy.

- *Sound:* Chant 'Fae' on the note of 'A'.

Each of these methods will cleanse your crystals, raising them to their highest vibration for optimum healing benefits.

## Crystal healing methods

There are a host of ways in which you can benefit from the healing energies of crystals:

- *Using crystals as tools:* Fairy healers often work with crystals when performing extraction (an ancient healing method that pulls unwanted energy out of the patient) or dreamweaving (performing healing by visiting the patient in the dreamtime and working on them in that state). Crystals also act as a bridge between worlds when journeying in the dreamtime (*see exercise below*).

- *Placing crystals on the body:* It is an ancient tradition for a fairy healer to wear crystals on their person.

Crystals can also be placed directly on the body, on a painful or troublesome spot. They can be placed on the chakras, which will energize and balance the natural flow of energy in and around us.

- *Placing crystals under your pillow:* If you do this, healing benefits will be brought to you while you are asleep. Certain crystals can help with insomnia, nightmares and psychic attacks, as well as dream recall and astral travel. You can programme a crystal to assist with any of these.

## Exercise: Journeying with crystals

Before you go to bed, consciously cleanse your body in the shower or bath. Light candles and treat the process like the sacred ceremony it actually is, for you are preparing for the dreamtime – a time when most people drift into an unconscious sleep, with no control over what happens. But you need not be unconscious during this time. During the dreamtime you become your soul essence and travel through time and space. There there are no limits to the worlds you can journey to and between. Time does not exist and you are able to meet your ancestors and future self – and remember it all.

❖ Before you fall asleep, in your mind's eye place a circle of bright light around yourself as protection and ask to be guided to wherever you wish to go, or to learn whatever it is you wish to know.

❖ For further protection, hold a crystal for journeying, such as black tourmaline, as you fall asleep.

❖ If you wish to heal another person in the dreamtime, hold a healing stone, such as green malachite.

❖ Keep a journal by your bed so that you can record your dreams. When you wake, interpret them according to what is happening in your life at the time.

---

### Crystal grids

You can also use crystals in the form of a grid. I used them in this way when I wanted to protect a natural beauty spot with a lake from an invasive refuse depot that had been built only a few hundred metres away. I tuned in to the nature spirits that inhabited the place and found it teeming with gnomes and dwarves. I agreed to build a crystal grid along the perimeter of the spot and went home to see which crystals wanted to sign up. Those who wished to be enlisted shone and sparkled enough to catch my eye and were taken back to the lake.

The stones knew exactly what they were there to do, and so I laid them out according to the plan that had been projected into my mind's eye by the dwarves.

When the crystal grid was complete, the energy was transferred from crystal to crystal, creating a 'force-shield' around the site to keep out the harsh energies of the newly built depot.

## Crystal meditation

Crystals are also wonderful tools for inducing and enhancing a meditative state. The quartz family are the most popular for this, particularly amethyst and clear, rose and smoky quartz, but any crystal can be used for meditation in accordance with its individual properties.

### Exercise: Meditating with crystals

❖ Take a crystal and hold it gently with your hands resting in your lap.

❖ Focus your attention on it.

❖ Notice its shape, form and colour. Notice its beauty.

❖ Close your eyes and become aware of your breathing.

❖ Breathe in deeply from your abdomen, then exhale slowly, blowing deliberately through your mouth.

❖ Continue breathing in this way until your mind is free of any thoughts.

❖ Now as you breathe in, feel your body overflowing with the blissful healing energies of the crystal.

❖ As you exhale, feel any tension in your body dissolving.

❖ Allow yourself to sink deeper and deeper into a meditative state.

❖ Feel your energy field expanding and filling with beautiful crystalline energies.

❖ Now imagine that you are becoming part of the crystal. Allow your energy to merge with that of the crystal. Become aware that you have the same life-force running through you.

❖ Allow yourself to enter your crystal and explore its magical kingdom.

❖ Feel its crystalline energy and enjoy a healing.

❖ Remain in your blissful meditative state for as long as you wish.

❖ When you are ready to return, become aware of your body and your contact with the Earth. Gently move your fingers and toes and notice your surroundings.

❖ Take a deep breath in and slowly open your eyes.

❖ Thank the spirit of the crystal and thank the dwarves for their guardianship of crystals and rocks.

## Seashells

Many healers recognize the benefits of working with crystals, but please don't underestimate the healing properties of seashells! Remember that shells have a direct connection with the creatures of the ocean and the sea itself. They have been cleansed by the reviving salt of the ocean, as well as imbued with the strength of sunlight and the magic of the moon and stars.

## Exercise: Healing with seashells

To set the scene for performing healing with seashells you may wish to play sounds of the ocean waves on a CD.

❖ Light a sea-salt 'flavoured' incense and some blue candles.

❖ Place carefully selected shells on your patient's chakras and call in some powerful mermaid energy by saying:

> *'Magical beings from oceans and sea,*
> *lend me your powers and assist me.*
> *Show me the ailments and where to place shells,*
> *through insight drawn from the water of wells.*
> *The healing begins from spirit to soul,*
> *health is restored – now fully whole!'*

❖ Imagine a strong golden light coming out of your hands. This is the healing light of the mermaids.

❖ Place your hands on each shell in turn and imagine the patient enjoying good health.

❖ When you have finished, offer the patient a glass of water. Give thanks for the healing that has come through you by saying to them, or asking them to say along with you:

> *'I give thanks to the waters of ocean and sea,*
> *and accept this healing most graciously.'*

## Fairy essences

Sometimes our energy isn't as high as we would like it to be. Other times the natural fairy in us can't handle being bogged down by the lower, often miserable, energies of those who refuse to open their hearts to the fairy realm. At such times we need a quick fix to feel that 'fairy thing' going on. Fairy essences are wonderful for such occasions and are so easy to make.

### Exercise: Making a fairy essence

You will need:

- tiny crystals, such as clear or rose quartz

- ionized water (you can buy this at a chemist's or simply use cold water that has previously been boiled)

- a 30ml opaque-coloured bottle with a spray top

- essential oils such as geranium, lemongrass and rose (this is my favourite concoction for fairy connection, but feel free to experiment and choose your own)

❖ Take the bottle and fill it three-quarters full with ionized water.

❖ Add in a couple of drops of pure alcohol. (Cheap vodka works well!)

❖ Now add 20 drops of geranium oil.

❖ Then 15 drops of lemongrass.

❖ Finally, 12 drops of rose oil.

❖ Now sprinkle the tiny crystals into the water.

❖ Twist the lid on tightly and shake the bottle.

Your fairy essence is now ready to spray into your aura and use for clearing a room, preparing a healing space and bringing in a vibration that is pure fairy joy!

## SUMMARY

• Fairies have shared healing knowledge with fairy doctors for centuries.

• Healing fairies resonate on an electric blue frequency.

• Crystals are members of the fairy realm and the wards of the dwarves.

• Each type of crystal has its own healing and restorative properties.

• Seashells are wonderful healing tools, being connected to the magical properties of the ocean.

• Spray fairy essences in your aura to protect yourself from harm and raise your vibration to *fairy*!

# Following the Fairy Path

*A fairy door has opened,*
*a giggle bids you follow.*
*Entranced, you take a fairy peek,*
*and join them in the hollow.*

This is where the magic really starts, as the fairies begin to weave aspects of your life into their own shining world.

So, give yourself a chance to be silent in order to hear the loving messages that they are trying to give you. Go out into nature and notice the beauty that is all around you. Be still, breathe and connect with the fae within. Here in this sacred place you will regain your balance and will be able to see with new fairy eyes.

Then go grab your dreams with both hands. Reach for the stars! Step fully into your power, as fairy energy surrounds you and a magical path unfolds before you. A wonderful world of freedom and magic awaits.

## Environmental fairy work

Some of the most important fairy work you are likely to undertake will be environmental. The fairy pathwalker is a healer, a counsellor, an ambassador for the spirits of nature and a guardian of our beloved planet. The Earth is becoming very uncomfortable at this time and we must ensure her – and our – future.

All the elements are affected:

- *Earth:* We are witnessing an unusual number of Earth tremors and quakes along faultlines. Pesticides, fertilizers and other poisons are polluting the land, and the Gnomes are having to work much harder to nurture the soil and ensure the healthy and plentiful growth of plants and crops.

- *Air:* The Sylphs are having to work harder than ever as the air becomes more and more polluted because of increasing industrialization.

- *Fire:* The fires of the sun are causing flares that affect all layers of the solar atmosphere.

- *Water:* Oceans are filled with plastics and poisons that are disrupting natural habitats and killing marine life. There is pollution from shipping, as well as from soil eroding during rainstorms and carrying with it agricultural fertilizers and pesticides. Eighty per cent of pollution of the marine environment comes from small land sources such as septic tanks and motor oil.

The fairies are counting on us to assist them in their roles at this time:

- We can help the Gnomes by recycling, picking up litter and growing vegetables, plants and flowers without the aid of synthetic materials.

- We can help the Sylphs by taking a look at our own carbon footprint. This includes all forms of commercial travel. How many unnecessary trips do you take in the car? We can also help by visualizing divine white light spreading through the skies, eliminating smoke, smog and pollution. Remember that whatever we imagine is carried out in the Otherworld, which will help it to manifest in this world.

- We can help the Salamanders by installing solar panels on our home to help combat greenhouse gas emissions and reduce our collective dependence on fossil fuel – thus helping out the Earth elementals as well!

- We can help the Undines by supporting marine clean-up groups such as Oceana.org and/or by visualizing clean and pure waters across the globe.

The energies on this planet are changing and can no longer support anything that is not in alignment or harmony with the natural world. This is why societies, countries and corporations that have grown fat on the back of lies and collective control are facing so many crises at the moment.

The truth is breaking through and the fairy mystic within you is beginning to stir...

Remember, it's your responsibility to inject some fairy magic into the world and it really does start with *you*.

What's the best way to begin?

## Make every day magical

Even though you may have felt a calling, you may not actually know what it is you are meant to do now. Why not treat every day as though you are walking through the pages of a fairy tale or starring in your own fairy movie?!

## Everyday magical activities

- Start the day by pulling a fairy card from an oracle deck to receive an insightful message.

- Take a sea-salt bath.

- Place crystals or shells on your chakra points for some fairy energy healing.

- Take a walk in nature.

- Sit against or hug a tree.

- Pick up litter on behalf of the fairies.

- Make wishes.

- Leave out little fairy gifts.

- Blow as one with the wind.

- Bless the rain.

- Bathe in the warmth of the sun.

- Dance barefoot on the grass.

- Become conscious of the elements you are using throughout your day, and remember to acknowledge the elementals who are working so hard behind the scenes.

Remember that whatever energies you are giving out, the fairies naturally receive. So share with them your joy, laughter and fun, and they will impart to you fairy wisdom.

A gateway has opened and you are invited to step through it into a world that has been waiting for you. You have an important life purpose and are here to shine brightly. Have faith, for there may be diversions along the way, but each is designed to give you the gift of experience that your soul requires to complete your mission.

Whenever the sun comes out to greet you or the moon shines upon you, a new glittering path will be revealed and the fairies urge you to take it. So go explore, investigate, pursue adventure and become the magic that you truly are.

As you start to live magically, magic will find you – and will guide you towards your very own...

### *Happily ever after*

*Awake at once! No time to wait.*
*The future calls, cannot be late.*
*A path that glitters is revealed –*
*follow, for your fate is sealed.*
*Seek, unlock the truth, be free*
*and walk towards your destiny.*

May you always fly with the fairies.

*Love and fae blessings,*

*Flavia Kate xx*

# Recommended Reading

If you wish to explore the magic further, here are some books and magazines that include some of the topics we've covered:

Conway, D. J., *Celtic Magic*, Llewelyn, 1990

Guyett, Carole, *Sacred Plant Initiations*, Bear and Company, 2015

Lily, Simon and Sue, *Healing with Crystals and Chakra Energies*, Hermes House, 2003

Meiklejohn-Free, Barbara, *The Shaman Within*, Moon Books, 2012

Sternfield, Jonathan, *Firewalking*, Berkshire House, 1992

Wells, David, *Your Astrological Moon Sign*, Hay House, 2012

*FAE* magazine: www.faemagazine.com

*Mermaids & Mythology* magazine: www.themermaidmagazine.com

# Acknowledgements

When you wish upon a star, your dreams come true...

To my real-life fairy godmother, Barbara Meiklejohn-Free, my dream-maker, soul sister and partner in all things magical, thank you for absolutely everything!

To my Pixie Pa and Wicked Stepmother, thank you for your love and support, and for believing!

To my fabulous fairy friends Sharon *Salamander* Sequoia, Kerry *Pixie* Doyle and KitKat, thank you so much for all your love and magical support.

To my beautiful fairy cat, Anubis, for accompanying me on the journey.

To lovely Amy and all the team at Hay House UK. Thank you so much for bringing the magic alive and for making a wish come true that was made upon a star 11 years ago.

A magical gateway has opened...